CHOSEN DAYS

Celebrating Jewish Festivals in Poetry and Art

שלמה

Chosen Days

Celebrating Jewish Festivals

in Poetry and Art

By David Rosenberg

With Decorations by Leonard Baskin

DOUBLEDAY & COMPANY INC., GARDEN CITY, NEW YORK, 1980

ACKNOWLEDGMENTS

For their invaluable help in shaping this book, I would like to thank my editors, Randall E. Greene and Shaye Areheart.

The poems in CHOSEN DAYS are interpretive translations made from the original biblical Hebrew texts. In "Who Can Despise a People with Women Like This?" I used the modern Hebrew reconstruction of A. Kahana, made from the surviving Judeo-Greek.

David Rosenberg

The author and the publisher express their appreciation to the following for permission to include excerpts from the material indicated:

Harper & Row, Publishers, for passages from: "Psalm 90," which appears in BLUES OF THE SKY. Copyright © 1976 by David Rosenberg, revised, reprinted, and appearing in this volume under the title "This Human Universe" by permission of Harper & Row.

"Chapter 23" and "Chapter 29," which appear in JOB SPEAKS. Copyright © 1977 by David Rosenberg, revised, reprinted, and appearing in this volume under the title "A Cloak of Pride Slid from My Shoulders" by permission of Harper & Row.

"Chapter 6," which appears in LIGHTWORKS. Copyright © 1978 by David Rosenberg, revised, reprinted, and appearing in this volume under the title "The Body of Memory" by permission of Harper & Row.

Schocken Books for "The Book of Judith," which appears in A BLAZING FOUNTAIN. Copyright © 1978 by David Rosenberg, revised, reprinted, and appearing in this volume under the title "Who Can Despise a People with Women Like This?" by permission of Shocken Books.

The author and publisher also express appreciation to the following periodicals for their publication of excerpts from CHOSEN DAYS: CELEBRATING JEWISH FESTIVALS IN POETRY AND ART: *Harper's Magazine* (January 1980), *Hudson Review* (Fall 1980), *The New Republic* (late 1980), *Response* (Summer 1980), *Menorah* (Fall 1980), and *Voices Within the Ark*, an anthology (Avon Books, 1980).

Library of Congress Cataloging in Publication Data
        Art director: Diana Klemin
Text copyright © 1980 by David Rosenberg
Decorations copyright © 1980 by Leonard Baskin
Library of Congress Catalog Card Number: 79-7906
ISBN: 0-385-14365-6
All rights reserved
Printed in the United States of America
First Edition

To Leslie

CONTENTS

INTRODUCTION

I A Family of Days

The intensity and concern, the demands and compassion of a family make the Hebrew Bible special among the world's books. Involved in the lives of real people, it is always listening in, insatiable in its hunger for true character. As a literature, it grew out of a body of experience no less alive today. It was lived by our parents in Europe, and it is lived by children in Israel today—as if it were written yesterday, its words steeped in the juices of body and thought that produce a passion for knowing.

Jewish festivals use particular events in the family-like history as illustrations of a *continuous* commitment. In many historical eras, Jews found themselves assimilating the world's dominant cultural modes while continuing to resist the myths that gave rise to them. The Torah (the Bible's first five books) was always an example of this resistance to the practices of the majority, yet still using and transforming the majority's cultural knowledge—and this linked Jewry in diverse cultures to each other like family. This wasn't a family against the world or out to win it; uniquely, they were a family who could not ignore the world—in fact, were dedicated to humanizing it while anchored in Jewish tradition.

The festivals themselves relate to each other as family, each one of a different age and character. In addition, with the exception of Hanukkah, all have biblical origins, though each was shaped by a different epoch. Together, they convey a sense of being at home in Time. Also, as a family of days, they convey a messianic realism, a belief in the eventual brotherhood of mankind on earth. Further, in the synagogue readings and home customs, they are occasions for involvement with the history of family life. And finally, the pluralism of the family is set before the unity of God—an absolute unity, often evoking the basic awareness that absolute truth is always beyond us.

Such relative truths as those with which we live cause us to need the nourishing of familial care.

Similarly, such a family relationship is depicted, in the Hebrew Bible, to be behind man's history, causing Jewish life to project the nature of family experience onto all relationships. Therefore, to the Jew, all relationships became subject to the covenant of that family—its *law*—but also subject to the compassion which holds that family together. This compassion, or loving-kindness in the biblical tradition, is derived from covenantal inspiration. To have made the notion of a contract an intimate pattern for personal relationships is almost as contemporary as today's best seller on selfhood, in which the term "covenants" is used to describe ideal psychological patterns of behavior. The integrity of the contract is at the root of civilization, and the projection of family feelings in the idiom of compassion has been a source of civilized hopes since Moses came down from the mountain.

The revelation of the covenant is thematically woven into the fabric of the year by the festivals. The festival days humanize the fear of the unknown by illuminating the continual process of change within time; the stability, via the covenant, is beyond time. So the fears of death and change are faced head on in the context of an earthly history and a family relationship which allows for a sharing of tragedy as well as joy. Space was given human dimension in the land of Israel, and time in the promise of a future for our children. The universe is not reduced to superstition and chance, as popular religions and sciences have tended to do. Instead, Judaic concepts allow the universe to be accepted—like an unknown, powerful neighbor—with the confidence inherent in family feeling.

Among the festivals, Passover is probably the major one today, fusing the physical reality of freedom with the spiritually liberating freedom of the desert revelation. Purim was like a close cousin to Passover as it expanded the sense of physical deliverance to a worldwide context, in which Jewish identity was already an established fact. Purim was a prooftext for the ongoing process of deliverance, just as Hanukkah was for the continual renewal of independence. So Hanukkah is a close cousin of Sukkot, the original festival of nation-building dedication. During the Roman persecutions, the Talmudic rabbis spoke of these younger cousins as the festivals that would endure in even the great, messianic age. By anchoring them to the future, the rabbis were de-emphasizing any idea of them as mere national celebrations.

The High Holy Days of Rosh Hashanah and Yom Kippur can be related to Shavuot by their common focus on revelation. The High Holy Days became a major observance sometime after the biblical Shavuot, growing out of an emphasis on individual self-realization. Since God spoke in the language of the Ten Commandments to each individual, Shavuot contained the seed of each individual's responsibility for revelation. So the process of Judaism's growing awareness in the world is felt as an embrace of its original integrity. The familial love in that embrace nourishes such continuing self-realization, until the feelings for freedom and love become intimately inseparable.

Thus, the family of days is lived out, as the Torah is read out loud, each with their particular stories (history), their customs (personality), and their special testimony about the integration of past, present, and future. In the presence of any one of them, as in the presence of a particular individual, we are directed to a feeling of interdependence.

II The Heritage Within Hearing

However scientific and adult we are, to speak about Jewish festivals requires speaking about God. Naturally this speech requires some use of the imagery that language allows. While the Bible uses the Hebrew language to convey the experience of "his" presence, we know that God is not a "he." It is our *feeling*—and not our idea—about God that is intensely personalized.

It is modern wisdom that God was first presented as a mythological phenomenon, as the pagan gods were. Yet the Hebrew God represented a rejection of mythology, because, instead of merely substituting new myth, the biblical tradition has remained a self-critical process, extending through centuries of history, prophecy, poetry, and commentary. Since God is beyond the powers of human knowledge, the cultural support of mythology (but not the imaginative feeling for it) is swept away. The way we come to sense the divine is through history and experience, and the Bible develops the spirit of truth at the core of Western civilization: a desire for empirical verification. This doesn't stop people in every age from using the Torah as if it were myth, but the penetrating criticism of the Prophets is always an example of the need for a demythologizing self-awareness.

In the same way, the Torah cannot be reduced to merely "literature," because it is the foundation of our awareness of myth itself. When we apply concepts of myth and idolatry in contemporary psychological idioms, we are exercising the same critical awareness the prophets began with. There are special readings from the Prophets, as with the rest of the Hebrew Bible, for each of the Jewish festivals. Like the Torah itself, the festivals are not based in myth but, as with the Song of Songs read at Passover, they transform remnants of ancient mythology. The myths behind Genesis were quarried for their ethical content, and then told with the unparalleled biblical ear for character delineation. Hence, the Torah *uses* myth—just as the great commentaries use legend and folklore—to articulate the awareness that we are ultimately anchored: in conscience, within; in history, without.

At home in the material universe, conversant with history, Judaism has focused on the understanding and application of what is within. Now that we've all learned that heaven is not "above" us, but that our planet is right up there in the midst of the heavens, we may find ourselves with new contexts of imagination, new mirrors to see ourselves in—but these mirrors and our images in them are still not ultimate answers. To interpret those images, we have the inner resources that have been honed in the process of interpreting the long Jewish heritage, in which the Talmud is but the major instance. Those resources have adapted to the widest range of developments in history, while continuing to refine the original core of Jewish experience.

This core is the Torah, containing the original distillation of the world of myth in which conscience was fully revealed. The Torah substantiates the existence of conscience, and proposes to perfect it, to project it into the world. The reality of conscience is felt with all the passion of the Torah's narrative and poetry. In the way the Torah approaches history and law, biblical imagination yields a fertile ground for discovery, for listening to the possibilities that are planted within us.

When Abraham responds to God's voice with the "Here I am" of Adam in Eden, I've translated it as "I am listening," because the emphasis now falls on a man's choosing to hear. These same words (a single word in Hebrew) are used by Isaiah to indicate his calling: an openness to a voice within (and within the tradition) that goes against the popular myths of the time. The Jewish festivals also place the emphasis on the present hearing.

The festivals, including Shabbat, have transmitted Jewish knowledge and literature since the Babylonian exile in the sixth century BCE, when synagogues and study houses probably originated. After the return to Israel, the scholars of the Sanhedrin studied the origins and customs of the festivals, and these studies led to major portions of the Talmud. By the first century CE, there were many books associated with each festival in the Talmud and Midrash. Soon afterward, the early rabbis added the biblical *megillot* (scrolls) as liturgy for each festival.

During the Second Jewish Commonwealth, which paralleled the rise of Rome, the Hebrew Bible was read in Israel in the early synagogues, according to a weekly sabbath schedule. As the Shabbat observance grew in importance, this reading served to diminish the popular legends that were often developed from superstition and mythic folklore. It was in this same way that historical elaboration of the biblical festivals had clashed with the mythic origins of the pagan harvest festivals: the weight of historical memory served to demythologize them.

So what the festival texts transmit, like the later prayers and poems, is a reverence for self-awareness and education. In themselves, the festivals have no mystical sacredness beyond their roots in the Torah. No Hebrew institution can be worshiped for itself—at the risk of idolatry—just as there are no sacred heroes. Yet to participate in the festivals, even if it is an active choice, requires acknowledging our dependence and facing up to our transience in time. The mythmaking desire to wholly create ourselves and to give our lives permanence is dethroned in the larger monotheistic perspective.

Instead, we find ourselves in the midst of a dynamic tradition, which continues to unfold. That tradition has placed the reading and hearing of texts at the center of the festivals and made the study of them as essential as religious observance. It is not mere ancient history being celebrated, not the Exodus of four thousand years ago, but the promise of a future that the festivals make present. When new lives are created, as was the recent immigrant experience in America and in Israel, that life still inherits the tradition of renewal.

I was asleep
but the soul within me
stayed awake

like my heart—true to a timeless rhythm
to which I still respond—
listen, a gentle knocking

like my heart's beating—
Open to me, my love
my purest image, sister, dove

all I can imagine—my head is drenched
with dew, all my memories
melt into you

In "PASSOVER":
from "All My Memories Melt into You"
(The Song of Songs)

CHOSEN DAYS

Celebrating Jewish Festivals in Poetry and Art

עקדה יצחק

BINDING OF ISAAC

ROSH HASHANAH

I AM LISTENING
   (The Book of Genesis)

TEARS THAT DISSOLVE INTO CRYSTAL-CLEAR VISION
   (The Book of Jeremiah)

THIS HUMAN UNIVERSE
   (The Book of Psalms)

THE BODY OF MEMORY
   (The Book of Isaiah)

I.

Rosh Hashanah means the head of the year. Unlike the secular New Year's Day, in which remnants of religious rituals still survive (for example, the driving off of evil spirits by loud noisemaking), the Jewish New Year's Day places pagan superstition in spiritual perspective. The Gregorian calendar's New Year's is a time for playing with old superstitions, such as reflections of pagan banqueting (drinking and party hats). But the Jewish Rosh Hashanah is a time for facing superstitious beliefs head on—and thoroughly resisting them in a rededication to a monotheistic visionary realism.

Naturally there were New Year's Days in pagan cultures before and during the early days of the people Israel. In great ancient civilizations such as Babylon, the New Year's Day was full of mythology, the day of a meeting of the gods. On the folk level, the day was tied to regeneration of nature spirits and the fertility gods of seasonal cycles. In either case, it was a day on which the fate of the future year was sealed and mere mortals were at the mercy of amoral gods. The Jewish Rosh Hashanah refuted this pagan world along with later cults of enlightenment and fatalism.

The significance of Rosh Hashanah as the second-most-holy day in the Jewish year was amplified by the early scholars of the Talmud. When the seasonal festivals of Passover, Sukkot, and Shavuot were cut off from the land of Israel, no longer observed by pilgrimages to Jerusalem and the rituals of the Temple (following 70 CE), their spiritual significance was reemphasized in terms of their original, biblical context. But the roots of the Days of Awe, Rosh Hashanah and Yom Kippur, continued to grow beyond their historical definitions. More than a day of renewal, Rosh Hashanah became a day of remembrance, yet not of a specific occurrence within human memory (except for the primordial first one, the first human's awareness of his or her creator). It became a day for honoring the gift of memory itself, and, through it, the creation of the world.

It was in the exile of the sixth century BCE that the Hebrew months were given their Babylonian names; prior to that, we know them by number and association, as in the Torah's designation of Rosh Hashanah as the first day of the seventh month. There, in the Bible, it was called a solemn memorial day, which was later interpreted as a day of judgment. But not simply judgment, in its ancient conjunction with fate, for the Jewish concept was infused with a sense of mercy. Where the god Marduk reigned in the natural world—annually resurrected on the Babylonian New Year's Day and married to his goddess—the Jewish realization of one God toppled such mythological machinery, imbuing Rosh Hashanah with a deeper spiritual perspective.

The key theme of Rosh Hashanah is the "kingship" of God, and awareness of that kingship divests sanctity of material power from all kings, earthly or otherwise. God is not king of this realm or of that, of this world or of that, but of creation itself: that ongoing process in which we wake every day, as our ancestors did and our children do. We do not enthrone God, as he is unchanging, beyond creation. His kingship is our divine metaphor for both the heights and the limits of human imagination, just as our personification of "him" is symbolic of our limited understanding. And yet, especially on Rosh Hashanah, we acknowledge that we are human. And on Yom Kippur we will reacknowledge that each of us remains imperfect, human.

The spiritual meaning of Rosh Hashanah needs to be understood in its relationship to Yom Kippur, the two festivals being known as the Days of Awe. On Rosh Hashanah the individual and nation are called by the sound of the *shofar*, the ram's horn, to face judgment. Since God is compassionate, we can turn to him in repentance. This turning, or returning, is the key theme of Yom Kippur, the Day of Atonement. On Rosh Hashanah, our awareness of this process, of our human fallibility, reveals our nakedness before God. Before we can begin to search out the truth within ourselves, we acknowledge God's kingship and thereby the grandeur of our capacity to know that truth exists. In the metaphorical sense, our judgment is written on Rosh Hashanah but not sealed until Yom Kippur, ten days later. That is why the custom of wishing "L'shana tova tikosaevu" ("May you be inscribed in the Book of Life for a good year") survives intact into our own day.

The theme of kingship is complemented in the liturgy by themes of remembrance and repentance. These themes are amplified in the special prayer book used on the Days of Awe, the Mahzor. The core of the Mahzor was collected in Talmudic times, not long after the destruction of the Second Temple (70 CE) and the beginning of the enforced exile from Israel—as decreed by the Romans (and accompanied by massacres) and lasting for almost nineteen centuries, though some Jews always managed to remain. In those days of the Talmud, also coinciding with the two hundred years of the Second Jewish Commonwealth, symbolic metaphors of heaven and resurrection were imaginatively drawn out. Yet the Jewish beliefs in an immortal soul and ultimate resurrection appear severely refined when compared to the wild and woolly imaginings characteristic of Hellenistic times.

The Second Jewish Commonwealth survived in a sea of Hellenistic culture, which dominated the Mediterranean world at that time. Many cults and sects arose during those days, complete with fashionably weird visions, apocalypses, and testaments. A free-flowing style with symbolic angels, miracles, and resurrections was as contemporary then as stream-of-consciousness recently was—we recognize both styles as cultural mediums for their times. What characterized Judaism then and characterizes it now is an ability to absorb changing styles through the ages, and the Mahzor records this journey through time: from the biblical origins of the Kedushah through prayers of Hellenistic times, from Roman-era hymns to medieval poems, and on up to modern additions. But the biblical religion itself did not change; rather, it was amplified and rearticulated, whether by commentary, prayer or moral tale. So Rosh Hashanah, which received the greatest degree of amplification during the Hellenistic age of lush metaphorical idioms, is today the Jewish festival most richly embellished with visionary imagery.

II.

The special Torah reading for the second day of Rosh Hashanah is the Binding of Isaac, from Genesis. The *haftarah* portion is a chapter from the prophet Jeremiah. We can date Jeremiah in the sixth century BCE; the portion from Genesis, though written down much later, describes a time almost twelve centuries before Jeremiah. Naturally the differences in style and content will yield some historical insight, and their juxtaposition helps to illuminate a deep tradition. Beyond that, these texts were chosen to shed light on the content of Rosh Hashanah, especially its universal significance: Israel's witness to the world. Since the second day of Rosh Hashanah recognizes Jewish communities far from Jerusalem, its liturgy is appropriate to the American experience.

There is a wealth of commentary on the Binding of Isaac. Two things in particular informed my version, "I Am Listening." First, contrary to my childhood understanding, Isaac was a mature youth in his twenties. An orthodox tradition reckons his age as high as thirty-three, so Isaac's understanding and acceptance of what transpires is crucial. He is not only submitting to the judgment of his father, but is aware of his father's submission as well. Therefore, this episode demonstrates the transmission of Abraham's dedication to God through his son.

We already know from the narrative that God has a hand in Isaac's birth—and we know from the outset that this is a test of Abraham's voluntary dedication. All of this enhances the poignancy of Abraham's loss were Isaac to die. But is it a cruel test? Not when we know beforehand that the nature of this test is to strengthen. We are hearing a text that is intensely dramatized so that we may feel ourselves present: it is our own faith that is being tested, and only the spiritually immature would dread God's judgment.

So, foremost, this portion of Genesis is a dramatization of God's mercy. Not his mercy toward Isaac, but toward ourselves—because we are the living descendants in the narrative and continue to listen and remember.

This leads me to the second insight I felt in the process of translating "I Am Listening": its symbolic representation of revelation. The Lord reveals a ram for the sacrifice, but first it is God's true desire that is revealed to Abraham by an angel's voice—Abraham remained open to it, he was listening. The emphasis is on that quality of dedicated openness, and on our present openness rooted in the original biblical revelation on "the mountain of the Lord."

When we read the Akedah (the Binding) as liturgy, we participate in an act of remembrance. On Rosh Hashanah, memory itself is redemptive. In "Tears That Dissolve into Crystal-clear Vision," the portion from Jeremiah, the analogy is deepened as God remembers Israel, evoked in a vision dramatizing his compassion. The poignance of this vision is framed by our awareness that it followed an act of judgment, as Israel was sent into exile. The nature of judgment is also raised to the visionary, and it not to be taken merely on its literal level. We can look at Israel today and say the prophecy still applies, just as we know that Jeremiah literally experienced the destruction of Jerusalem. But that is a false interpretation, reducing history to simplistic allegorizing, because it misses the depth of Jeremiah's vision as well as the pertinence of Rosh Hashanah. All that Jeremiah reveals stems from the awareness of compassion bound up in God's judgment.

As God remembers Ephraim (a term of endearment for Israel, the northern kingdom); as Jeremiah remembers a mother of Israel, Rachel; and as we remember to listen to his words, recalling the "immeasurable richness" of revelation in the desert at Sinai, then: "vision is your reward/ there is new life for your labor, remembrance/ in the presence of children." The key is a "listening" and a "returning/ remembering in the turning/ trusting in the memory." Just as Ephraim and Rachel are not concepts but breathing, tender presences of God—via Jeremiah's poetry—so the vision of redemption, rooted in the blessing of Abraham's descendants, is felt in the wide-open eyes of children.

As the beginning of "Tears That Dissolve into Crystal-clear Vision" evokes the revelation at Sinai, "This Human Universe" is the psalm prefaced "A Prayer of Moses, a man of God," also recalling the revelation. Remembrance of Abraham is echoed "in the open-eyed grace of children." The image of God's kingship is omnipresent in the psalm, as the eternity of his dominion is contrasted with the shifting sands of individual and national existence. Psalm 90 is read in the Rosh Hashanah Musaf (special festival service). As God is asked to "return/ and forgive us," the fault we're made to feel most deeply lies in the failure to be aware of his kingship's grandeur, to be "unawed," and to forget our role as "returning witnesses" in this human universe: a failure of vision.

The central motif of God's kingship is at the heart of Jewish prayer in the Kedushah (Sanctification), part of every synagogue service. The ancient verses are on the lips of the seraphim as they sing God's praises in Isaiah's throne vision, in the days of Solomon's Temple. Especially on Rosh Hashanah, its recitation takes the form of symbolically standing before the vision of God's throne and blessing *him*: "Holy/ Holy/ Holy/ is the Lord/ beyond/ all that is—/ and filling the world/ with the substance of light/ unfolding creation."

"The Body of Memory" is from the sixth chapter of the Book of Isaiah. The concrete date in the time of King Uzziah (eighth century BCE) is contrasted with the "unfolding creation" of God's kingship, reinforcing the creation and kingship themes of Rosh Hashanah. The style of Isaiah's vision is realistic, so that we can easily imagine him standing in the Temple's sanctuary on a Day of Awe. As the sanctuary walls become the legs of the throne, the holy incense becomes "white smoke/ clouds." When the Lord asks for a witness, Isaiah finds himself saying, "here am I," the same word in Hebrew that Abraham answers God with. In Genesis, I translated the sense of that word as "I am listening," but here the context is so clearly one of listening and witness that the resonance of the Hebrew speaks for itself.

The theme of turning (repentance), leading toward Yom Kippur, where it is the dominant theme, is raised in the vision of Israel one day being moved "to turn and become/ wholly human again." The ultimate majesty of God's kingship is fully revealed in contrast to the words of temporal kings, forgotten and "wiped out like royal contracts etched in sand." The sanctification of God's sovereignty over creation is fully realized on Rosh Hashanah. It is the "birthday of the world."

I AM LISTENING
(The Book of Genesis)

And some time later
after these things had happened
God tested Abraham
speaking to him
"Abraham"
"I am listening" he answered

And God said
please take your son
whom you love
dear as an only son
that is, Isaac
and go out to the land of Moriah

There you will make of him a burnt offering
on a mountain of which I will tell you
when you approach

And Abraham rose early in the morning
saddled his donkey
took two of his young workers
to go with him and his son, Isaac
having already split the wood
for the burnt offering
and he started out for the place
of which God had spoken
to him

It was on the third day
Abraham looked out in the distance
and there, afar, was the place
and Abraham turned to his young men
you will wait here by yourselves
with the donkey
while the youth and I go on ahead
to worship and then
we will return here to you

Abraham took the wood for the burnt offering
laying it upon Isaac, his son
and in his own hands he took the flint
and the knife
then the two walked on together

At last Isaac spoke to his father, Abraham
"Father"
"I am listening, my son"
We have the flint and the wood
to make the fire, but where is the lamb
for a burnt offering?

Abraham answered
God will reveal his lamb, my son
for the burnt offering
and the two walked on together

And they approached the place
of which God had spoken
there Abraham prepared an altar
set the wood upon it
then bound his son, Isaac
and laid him there, on the altar
lying upon the wood

Abraham reached out
with his hand, taking
the knife, to slaughter
his son

But a voice was calling to him
an angel of the Lord, calling
from out of heaven
Abraham, Abraham
I am listening, he answered

Do not lay your hand upon the youth
you will not do anything to him
for now I know yours is an integrity
dedicated to God
not holding back your son
your dear one, from me

Then Abraham looked around and there
behind him
its horns tangled up in a thicket
a ram had appeared

And Abraham went over to it
carrying the ram to the wood
for a burnt offering
instead of his son

The name of that place
was given by Abraham, meaning
"The Lord reveals"
and today we still say
"The mountain of the Lord
is revelation"

The Lord's angel spoke again
calling to Abraham from heaven
By myself I have sworn
says the Lord
as by yourself you have acted—
have not held back even your son
dear to you as an only one—
and for this thing you are immeasurably blessed
and your seed multiplied
immeasurable as the stars in the sky
and as the grains of sand by the sea

For this thing you have done
your descendants will walk freely
through the gates of their enemy
and all the nations of the earth
will feel themselves blessed
one day, knowing
that your descendants thrive
living among them—
for it was you who listened
and heard my voice

So Abraham returned to his young men
they turned and started out together
for Beersheba
and Abraham stayed there, in Beersheba.

(Chapter 22:1–19)

TEARS THAT DISSOLVE
INTO CRYSTAL-CLEAR VISION
(The Book of Jeremiah)

Listen to words the Lord has spoken:
A people discovered grace
when they had run away

a consoling treasure
when they had escaped an enslaving power
into the desert

immeasurable richness in front of their eyes
opening their hearts and minds
when you had looked only for rest, Israel

the Lord reveals his words to me
as he was then, in that desert
ages ago, saying

a love that lasts forever
I revealed to you
and you always will carry that loving-kindness

the love that drew you to me
will rebuild your nation
will draw you home, dear Maiden Israel

again you will fasten on timbrels
leading the dance   keeping time
to the rhythm of seasons

again you will clothe the mountains with vineyards
the hills of Shomron will sparkle
with the jewelry of vines

and you will live to pluck the fruit
to raise it to your lips
to praise it, singing

for there will be a day
when watchmen on the hills of Ephraim
will shout, the way is clear

we may go up to Zion
the mountain of vision
walking in the presence of the Lord

for these are the Lord's words:
raise a song to your lips for Jacob
let the startled nations hear it

let their watchmen turn to it
on every hilltop listening post
of the world

let it be music to their ears:
Am Yisrael chai
the people of Israel live

I am bringing them back from the north
and gathering them
from the ends of the earth

look, the blind and the lame are returning
women heavy with child, and yes
even those already feeling birth pangs

a great congregation is coming
weeping openly, and among them little cries
of newborn infants—sweet and gracious tears

and I will lead them beside rushing waters
on fertile ground, on soil so smooth
not a foot will stumble on the way

their path is straight, clear before them
for I am Israel's father
Ephraim my firstborn son

nations of the world, listen
to the word that is the Lord's
turn and tell it to the islands

islands, send it to the coasts
the one who scattered Israel
is a shepherd who never sleeps

and will bring them back
gathering his flock tenderly
unchanging as the sea

for the Lord has redeemed Jacob
paid the ransom into the worldly hand
that was too strong for him

they will come home with songs
singing from the mountaintop
that is Zion

the land will be beautiful in their eyes
the earth's goods abundant
in their hands

the fullness of their hearts
will reap wheat
and wine and oil

flocks of sheep
giving birth to healthy lambs
vigorous herds of cattle

and the people will take root
thrive and stretch themselves
like a watered garden

they will not be confined
not imprisoned in exile again
not steeped in sadness

the maiden will dance unashamedly
young men and old men
will join in together

I will turn their sighing
into breaths of excitement
their sadness into blushes of joy

and they will relax by fountains
of imagination, clearing the air
of dank grief

their mourning changed into music
of birds alighting in trees, by windows
thrown open to new mornings

the priests will have their arms full
with gifts for the sacrifice
the hunger of the people will be filled

with the goodness of the world
and their hearts thrown open
to hear these words again

like fresh air to comfort them
for the Lord has given his word—
just as now you hear his words:

listen, a voice sobbing in Ramah
bitter weeping, open
inconsolable

Rachel mourns her children
refusing all comfort, all soothing
all her hope gone blind:

her children gone—
yet these are the Lord's words:
your voice will cease its weeping

your eyes brighten behind the tears
that dissolve into crystal-clear vision
of the children alive

returning home
from the lands of enemies
from beyond anguish to hope revived

vision is your reward
there is new life for your labor, remembrance
in the presence of children, eyes wide open

turning to the future
that is also yours
within the borders of a reality

and beyond them your descendants
are walking freely
by the strength of an unfailing imagination

an unbroken integrity
a listening   dedicated
to the words that bade them live.

As I have heard Ephraim crying
as I hear him rocking in grief:
my heart has been trained

like a wild bull, an unbroken calf
all my desire set on returning
remembering in the turning

trusting in the memory
for you are the Lord
and were always my God

and when I opened my eyes in exile
my stomach turned, I knew my loss
and when I repented and learned

to bear the burden
and when I knew I had been tested
I broke down, I struck my forehead

aware of my arrogance
ashamed of the ignorance
blinding my youth

and I lived to face it
to blush with the disgrace
to embrace my past

Is Ephraim not my dear one
says the Lord
dear as an only child

that whenever I speak of him
I am filled with remembering
and my heart goes out to him

to welcome him back
to receive him with love
with mercy, says the Lord

mark your path well
plant guideposts and road marks
set your desire by the highway

your thoughts to the road leading home
turn back on it, my Maiden Israel
come back to these your cities.

(Chapter 31)

THIS HUMAN UNIVERSE
(The Book of Psalms)

Lord, you are our home
in all time
from before the mountains rose

or even the sun
from before the universe
to after the universe

you are Lord forever
and we are home
in your flowing

you turn men into dust
and you ask them to return
children of men

for a thousand years
in your eyes
are a single day

yesterday
already passed
into today

a ship in the night
while we were present
in a human dream

submerged
in the flood of sleep
appearing in the morning

like new grass
growing into afternoon
cut down by evening

we are swept off our feet
in an unconscious wind
of war or nature

or eaten away
with anxiety
worried to death

worn-out swimmers
all dressed up
in the social whirl

you see our little disasters
secret lusts
broken open in the light

of your eyes
in the openness
penetrating our lives

every day melts away
before you
our years run away

into a sigh
at the end
of a story

over in another breath
seventy years
eighty—gone in a flash

and what was it?
a tinderbox of vanity
a show of pride

and we fly apart
in the empty mirror
in the spaces between stars

in the total explosion of galaxies
how can we know ourselves
in this human universe

without expanding
to the wonder that you are
infinite lightness

piercing my body
this door of fear
to open my heart

our minds are little stars
brief flares
darkness strips naked

move us to see your present
as we're moved to name each star
lighten our hearts with wonder

return
and forgive us
locking our unconscious

behind the door
and as if it isn't there
as if we forget we're there

we walk into space unawed
unknown to ourselves
years lost in thought

a thousand blind moments
teach us when morning comes
to be moved

to see ourselves rise
returning witnesses
from the deep unconscious

and for every day lost
we find a new day
revealing where we are

in the future and in the past
together again
this moment with you

made human for us
to see your work
in the open-eyed grace of children

the whole vision unlocked
from darkness
to the thrill of light

where our hands reach for another's
opening to life
in our heart's flow

the work of this hand
flowing open
to you and from you.

(Psalm 90)

THE BODY OF MEMORY
(The Book of Isaiah)

It was the year King Uzziah
died and the year
I saw the Lord

as if sitting in a chair
the true throne
as it was very high

so high
the train
of his robe flowed down

to fill the Temple
where I was standing
the sanctuary

seraphic beings   burning
shone around him
six wings

each had six wings
two covering the face
enfolding it

two covering the torso
and enfolding the sex
of its body

and two unfolded
in space
flying

and each was calling
to each other
and the words were saying

a chorale   a fugue
an endlessly unfolding
hymn

Holy   Holy   Holy
is the Lord   beyond
all that is—

and filling the world
with the substance of light
unfolding creation—

the doors the windows the foundation
were shaken
moved by each voice calling

singing out
and the House was filling
with white smoke

clouds
and I heard myself
I was saying

Oh my God!
this is the end of me
my lips are a man's

unholy
I live among men and women
who give their lips falsely

give their lips to darkness
and now my eyes are given
blinding truth

inner and outer   the one
king: Lord beyond all—
and I'm uncovered   primitive

in horror of my darkness
in terror of inhuman space
exposed to a private death

totally vulnerable on the surface
of earth's
material matter . . .

then one of the seraphim
flew toward me
a live coal in his hand

a fire from the interior
of the earth
the core of my being

it was a burning stone
from the fire
on the altar

with the priest's tongs
he reached in the holy altar
and took it

and touched my lips
with it
and he was saying

you are seeing
the purifying fire of creation
burn up your past

and abstract fear and guilt
of light   of losing yourself
your small and only light

now abstraction turns concrete
on your lips
to feel the universe

the private guilt gone
purged   lanced
like a boil

erupted around your body . . .
and I was clean
and whole

and I heard the voice
of my creator
it was saying

whom will I send
to be a witness—
here am I   send me

I heard myself saying
and he said
go and say to this people

hear over and over
and understand nothing
look again and again

and again you don't see
the whole body:
of language, sound

of action, history
of memory
imagination

of matter, light
they can't even feel
the energy inside them

the material of their being
and you will make their hearts harder
like ignorant fists of matter

and their ears
heavy earrings for their mind
and their eyes shut

like a censor's eyes
before a naked soul
in front of them

their thoughts become glinting swords
to hide their narrowness
to reflect away light

they will stay out late
like stubborn children
bleary-eyed

heaven forbid they should see
with their eyes clear
hear with open ears

and understand by feeling
with that sacred metal cow
of their heart

and so be moved
to turn and become
wholly human again

how long I said how long
this shell this wall
and he was already saying

until cities have fallen
to the ground   not a house
with a person or statue standing

countryside a wasteland
until this king has driven men
away   the whole country

blown down like a primitive pile of stones
some forgotten sacred place
wiped out like royal contracts etched in sand

even the promise of a remnant of survivors
will slip from mind
like the hollow ring of a cliché

like leaves from a blighted oak
ripped in a hard wind
crumpled as the tree falls

the pages of that high pride
the record of its worldy dealings
will be smooth as a stump

the stump
the holy seed
remains.

(Chapter 6)

JONAH

YOM KIPPUR

THE BOOK OF JONAH

ARCHAEOLOGIST OF DAWN
(The Book of Isaiah)

A CLOAK OF PRIDE SLID FROM MY SHOULDERS
(The Book of Job)

I.

Yom Kippur means the day of atonement, but as the holiest day of the year it has acquired deeper resonance. After Israel's return from Babylonian exile, much of Yom Kippur's significance reinforced its Temple ritual. That ritual became imbued with universal relevance due to the creative expansion of Judaism. Hence, just as the experience in Babylon provided Israel with keen insight into worldly power, the tradition of Judaism was similarly reinterpreted with worldly insight. Furthermore, while other cultures had days of penitence and judgment, Yom Kippur became, uniquely, a day of judgment *and compassion*.

The legendary tradition of Yom Kippur uses poetic imagery of a heavenly tribunal, an allegory of God as judge and Israel as guilty penitent. This same type of imagery was employed by the prophets, when the poetic (and political) nature of their prophecy was clearly understood. In the portion from Isaiah read on Yom Kippur, the prophetic perspective on scripture and ritual is unfolded, in which literal and simplistic interpretations are judged to be corrupt. This chapter from Isaiah was probably written during the exile in Babylon, though it grows out of insights similar to those held by the original Isaiah in the eighth century BCE.

In addition, the ascendancy of Yom Kippur to be the most important event in the Jewish year parallels the rising emphasis on individual participation. Specifically, the holiday contends that the one God of creation works within men and women, not merely by external events. Did Israel not leave pagan fortune-tellers far behind, using prophecy instead to interpret the spiritual relationship between God and men, between itself and its witness to the world? Then, Yom Kippur focuses on the individual's vulnerability before God, and his opening to the divine spark within him.

As for the allegorical richness of Yom Kippur, it grew in each succeeding period of Jewish history. The Kol Nidre prayer, ushering in Yom Kippur, expands the symbolism of a tribunal. The final service, with its imagery of heavenly gates closing, was embellished by cabalistic tradition. Yet, to take all the imagery literally would be a corruption of Jewish insight. So, on Yom Kippur we confront this basic ground of Judaism openly, confessing our ignorance, our imperfection, our selfishness and self-deceptions. We affirm our capacity for love by searching out forgiveness. Therefore, on Yom Kippur we are made awesomely aware of love's power and its promise of redemption—balancing the solemn aspect of the Yom Kippur holy day by this underlying cause for celebration.

The Yom Kippur attributes—especially the twenty-four-hour fast—which seem to describe a day of guilt and remorse, were reinterpreted from earlier traditions. Essential among them, fasting heightens our spiritual awareness, our perspective on material pride, and our identification with the deprived and hungry. Attention to prayer and meditation is so consuming that we become critically aware of the power of speech in our humanness. And Judaism's heritage is based on this power: the hearing and the transmission of vision and wisdom, history and legend, imagination and ethics. It is the creative imagination which is at the core of resistance to superstition and idolatry, and that imagination is expressed through language: the books, commentaries, and tales. In the moral sphere, the Talmud regards the sins of speech as worse than those of action, based on the awareness of speech and the articulation of thought as the gifts that allow us to be fully human.

Finally, one of the early, creative translations of the Bible, from Hebrew into Aramaic, made in the second century BCE by Onkelos, translates what seems literally to say "And man became a living soul" into the interpretative "And man became a speaking spirit." In the same way, Yom Kippur's literal Temple rituals, the most awesome of any Jewish festival, became translated into Yom Kippur observance as narrative—describing the ancient Temple service and the special role of the high priest.

On Yom Kippur man confronts God after having accounted for his failures toward other men. That is all behind him when he stands naked before God, as if he were already dead. Dead, because he's alone; and in either case, in need of compassion. This is the divine compassion, mirroring the ethics of loving-kindness between men, that is felt with a love as strong as death.

II.

"The Book of Jonah" and "Archaeologist of Dawn" are the two haftorahs for Yom Kippur day. Isaiah is read in the morning, but the prophet Jonah, read in the afternoon, bears the more subtle and expansive relationship to Yom Kippur. The Book of Jonah contains a lesson in *teshuvah* (turning) and in God's universal presence. It also contains a lesson in forgiveness, divine and human. And it is this lesson of compassion, felt in the sense that God in his omnipotence is *above* kingship, that I've found the most crucial in my interpretation.

The book begins like a typical book of a prophet, with the call to witness. But in place of Jonah's words we are suddenly in the realm of narrative—the prophet is now humanized, his sins and failings characterized as bluntly as if he were any man. That, of course, is all that he is, and his book of prophecy comes close to putting every man and woman in the place of a prophet. On Yom Kippur, we are as alone in the crowd as a prophet, yet as much a part of the community of Israel as a prophet called to speak to it.

Jonah isn't called to speak to Israel but, rather, Nineveh, symbolic of the cosmopolitan, pagan world. And he flees Israel as well as his calling to Tarshish, the symbolic frontier of the known world. While it appears we have a fantastic tale or allegory unfolding before us, there is an essential difference between this book and the numerous legends and tales of similar date (around 400 BCE) recalled in the Midrash. Jonah will indeed use "fantastic" imagery, such as the fish, the plant, and the naïve Ninevites, but what remains most pertinent is the first surprise: this is prophecy *about* prophecy. As such, it is not so unusual a genre in Jewish literature—it is as familiar as *aggadah* (telling), the most popular form of commentary on the Bible in the Jewish tradition. In this book, we have a commentary on *all* the prophets, in the form of *aggadah*.

Beyond the narrative itself, the primary subject of Jonah as commentary is biblical language itself, particularly the language of prophecy and prayer. Both the narrative prose and the poetry of the prayer in Chapter 2 are a tour de force of language, contrasting the power of parable with lame literalism, the penetration of aggadic commentary with blind fanaticism. Those who want easy answers and explanations, who want to evade the difficulty of Yom Kippur, are sharply attacked in Jonah. The superficial, literal understanding of the Torah—understanding the surface meaning of the words but not their resonance—is contrasted with the emotional understanding required. It is deep, emotional truth (not surface truth) which is plumbed in Jonah, just as the hypocrisy of outward repentance and observance is criticized in the other prophetic portion read on Yom Kippur (from Isaiah).

Jonah uses many terms similar to Isaiah, and turns them inward, personalizes them. For example, the familiar word for "call," in the sense of a prophet's words (also used as "cry in its ear," since it is a word used of *human* conversation), is the same word used by the captain of the ship in the more mundane act of waking the napping Jonah. And the most emphatic contrast is its use by Jonah in his personal prayer within the fish's belly, compared to his relatively impersonal role as a prophet calling to Nineveh. This is one of many instances in which the language parallels the drama of Jonah finding himself in the turning to—rather than leaving—his difficult God.

Unlike the simplistic, capricious gods of the foreigners, who may be appeased with unquestioning rituals such as animal sacrifices, Jonah's God is concerned with humanity, rather than his personal cult and domain. Hence, the lesson revealed to Jonah in the last chapter is one of compassion—it's not Jonah's unquestioned obedience that is desired, but his openness, his conscious sense of self. Crudely put, Jonah discovers his identity in the personal and emotional nakedness of his prayer within the belly of death. Ensuing adventures in his role as prophet symbolically reinforce this.

The language of his prayer within the fish's belly, a womblike entombment, is markedly different from the narrative—its poetic and stylized language is clearly metaphorical, emphasizing the passionate imagination of open feeling. This poetry parallels the metaphorical imagery of fish and plant in the drama.

Parallelism is the dominant technique of biblical poetry. On its simplest level, parallelism is a form of repetition in which a slight change in words or image produces resonance. The Book of Jonah is like a commentary on this technique, as it uses the same words repeatedly in different contexts. Take the Hebrew word for "big" or "great"—this same word is applied to the fish, to the city of Nineveh, and to the hurricane. Clearly, a giant whale is uncalled for in understanding this book, as is a vision of a metropolis so huge it takes three days to walk across. Not that such delightful images are conjured up, but that the *literalness* of the words are secondary to the emotional depth of the context. The poet who set down the Book of Jonah used a commonplace form of biblical style so that the contrast between literal style and figurative imagery was most pronounced. As Jonah learned the lesson of compassion and of his error in taking God's call to him too literally (as if he could escape it by crossing a border, which is what was "literally" required of him in the call to Nineveh), we learn the Yom Kippur lesson of compassion. It's not the castor-oil plant that is the object lesson in the last chapter, but imagination itself: if we have the courage and openness of heart to imagine this scene, then we have felt an aspect of God's presence in creation. A presence we are refusing to hide from on Yom Kippur.

So the language of Jonah constantly surprises us. Jonah is "vomited" out of the fish onto the land of Israel just as that same word is normally employed by the prophets in sensing the opposite: the exile of Israel from its land. (It's probable that Jonah was composed in the fourth century BCE when the return from exile to the land was already an established fact.) Likewise, the emphasis on the human content of ritual, on the Jewish *transformation* of such pagan practices as vowing, sacrificing, mourning, and decrees, is everywhere present as aggadic commentary in the Book of Jonah. The great contrast between pagan fortune-telling (as in the "casting lots" of the sailors) and Jewish prophecy strikes us in our ears as well as our hearts. So this dating would place the composition of the Book of Jonah in an era paralleling the rising prominence of Yom Kippur as the holiest festival day.

Somewhat later, in the Talmud, prophetic awareness is made concrete in the emphasis on doing good deeds (*mitzvot*). Yet the visible trappings of religious and ethical observance, or their performance by rote, is criticized in the same terms as the prophets'. Referring to the Book of Jonah, the Mishnah says, ". . . of the people of Nineveh it is not said: And God saw their sackcloth and their fasting,[1] but: 'And God saw their works, that they turned from their evil way.' "[2] The Talmud points out the inward *turning* (*teshuvah*) over and against the observance.

Here is one, last example of Jonah as aggadic commentary on linguistic conventions of biblical prophecy, prayer, and narrative. The words the Ninevite king uses in Chapter 3, echoing the ship captain's words in the great hurricane, are "perhaps the God will relent and spare us"—reflecting the poignancy of the same words used in the Book of Samuel when King David prays for the life of his son by Bathsheba.[3] Just as Jonah's drama emphasizes God's compassion more than his judgment, the power of kings is compared with God's figurative kingship. God's compassion, and our reflection of it in acts of loving-kindness, reveal the imaginative use of "royal" imagery to demonstrate a higher level of understanding and spiritual insight. His presence in creation, his concern for all of it, even for plant and animal, reveals the centrality of a felt truth: we *feel* in his presence, the feeling lies within us, and never mind that "he" is not a "he," or that "his" words are ours, for that would be the ultimate literal blindness. Jonah's feeling for the plant demonstrates both the heights and the limits of imagination; by contrast, how limitless is God's compassion.

"Archaeologist of Dawn" attacks the conventions of observance empty of feeling. In the order of the Yom Kippur service, this portion of the Book of Isaiah is read in the morning, before the afternoon reading of Jonah, establishing the prophetic dimension that prepares us for Jonah's subtleties. Not that Isaiah is less sophisticated; on the contrary, his poetry is richer and more profound for its directness. The contrast between the shallowness of convention and the depth of vision is placed squarely within the breast of each individual.

In terms of the prophets, our vision will go only as far as our emotions are rooted in the judgment and compassion of creation. "Lift your voice/ like a horn/ to your lips"—observance, like the blowing of the ancient ram's horn, is a re-creation of life, and such rituals as prayer, fasting, and soul-searching can only be meaningful if they connect to everyday inner needs for awareness and compassion.

Once again, the theme struck on Rosh Hashanah returns in the "here I am" of this Isaiah chapter. But this time, on Yom Kippur, it is the Lord who is listening, who acknowledges his presence in the voices addressed to him, and

[1] (Jonah, 3:10).

[2] (Ta'anit, II:1; translated by Henry Malter, 1929, recently reissued in paperback—Jewish Publication Society, 1978).

[3] (II Samuel 12).

who answers with a compassionate "Here I am" or "I am listening." And "sing out openly/ and the Lord returns/ your voice." The result of our actions in turning to him, of "a soul undressed by kindness," is a renewed awareness of the "infinite light of reality," something the philosopher Franz Rosenzweig[4] called "the presence of eternity in time."

Because of the expansive framework of tradition, every Jewish text we use increases our perception of time, reminding us of a time past, of our present, and an anticipation of a time future. This Isaiah chapter reminds us of a time when the emphasis was shifting to individual awareness and communal observance, a time when Judaism survived and grew in spite of the nation's and the Temple's destruction. We're reminded of the flourishing religion of the Second Commonwealth, some centuries later, when Yom Kippur became the year's holiest day. And we are reminded of Judea's destruction by the Romans, and then the spiritual creativity of the early rabbis in editing the Yom Kippur texts. As these dates in history parallel the rises and falls of Greece and Rome, our awareness turns to the Western world, resting uneasily on those fallen pillars, and we who appear to have survived the twentieth century have already absorbed a preview of its fall.

---

[4] *The Star of Redemption* (Boston: Beacon, 1971).

Chapter 1

And the word of God came to the prophet Jonah
saying to him, Jonah ben Amittai: rise
go to Nineveh, the great city
and cry in its ear
because its hard heart stands out before me
like an open sore

Jonah rose, but to go instead
west to Tarshish: far away
out of the Lord's presence
to the ends of the earth, for good measure

Jonah went down to foreign Jaffa
found a ship going all the way to Tarshish
bought a one-way ticket
(paid in cash on demand)
went below like any other passenger
as the crew set sail for distant Tarshish
away from the Lord, out of his demanding presence

But the Lord threw a great wind
over the sea—a hurricane so great
the ship thought she'd be broken to pieces
all the sailors were scared to death
each trembling soul
crying to one god or another
then throwing all the cargo overboard
to lighten the load

Meanwhile Jonah, having already lain down
in the hold below, was fast asleep
the captain himself came down to him
and cried in his ear: what does this mean
this sleep of ignorance—rise
cry to your god
perhaps the god will turn his ear
and kindly spare us our death

Among the sailors each consulted his neighbor
and agreed: we must cast lots
revealing the source of this bitter fortune
so they cast lots, fortune continuing to unfold
as Jonah drew the cast lot

Turning to him they said: now tell us—
now that you've brought your bitter fortune
on all our heads—why are you here?
where did you come from?
what country, what people
do you belong to?

And he answered: I am a Hebrew
and I tremble before the Lord
God in heaven, creator of this sea
as well as dry land

And the men were struck with a great terror
their lips trembling as they asked: what
is this bitter fortune you've created?
because the men already knew Jonah's fear
of the Lord—of being in his presence
he has told them as much

And they asked: what can we do
for you, that might calm the sea
around us? for the sea was growing
into a great hurricane

And he said: lift me up, like a sacrifice
throw me into the sea
this will calm the sea for you
it was on account of me, I'm sure
this great hurricane surrounds you

But the men desperately rowed for dry land
yet couldn't—the sea grew even more
into a great hurricane

And they cried to the Lord
Please Lord hear us
we don't want to die for this man's soul!
along with him—please don't hold us guilty
of spilling his blood into the sea
for you are the Lord who has created
this fortune unfolding here

And they lifted Jonah up, like a sacrifice
and threw him into the sea

Suddenly the sea stopped its raging
the men trembled in awe

a great fear of the Lord engulfed them
right there
they slaughtered a sacrifice, sacrificing to him
they cried vows, vowing to him.

Chapter 2

And a great fish was waiting
the Lord had provided
to swallow Jonah

And Jonah was a long time
within the fish body
three days three nights

And Jonah prayed to the Lord
within the mothering fish body—
he prayed to his God, saying

I cried out within my despair
I called to the Lord and he answered me
I implored him within the belly of death itself

Yet he heard my voice—
I was flung into the abyss
swept into the sea's bottomless heart

Devoured by rivers
all your waves and walls of water
fell over me

And I was saying I am lost
cast away, driven out
of your presence, from before your eyes

How will I see
your holy Temple again
if I am gone?

Water was all around me
penetrating to my soul: I was almost gone
devoured by a flood

Seaweeds were tangled
around my head
I sank to the depths

I went down to the roots
of mountains
the earth shut her gates

Behind me
it was the end of the world
for me—and yet

From destruction you brought me to life
up from the pit
Lord my God

My soul was ebbing away within me
but I remembered the Lord
and my prayer came up to you

Up to your holy Temple
as if I were there
in your presence

Those who admire mists of illusion
to hide their fears
abandon the compassion of openness

But I with a thankful voice, not fearing
will make of sacrifice a thanksgiving
I will pay with gladness every vow I make

It is the Lord who delivers us
alive
he is the captain of our praises

I will pay my fare gladly
I am his
precious cargo

And the Lord spoke to the fish
and it vomited Jonah out
onto dry land.

Chapter 3

And the word of God came to the prophet Jonah
for the second time, saying: rise
go to Nineveh, the great city
and cry in its ear
with the words I give you to cry

Jonah rose, and went to Nineveh
as the word of God had said
now Nineveh was a great city

even in God's eyes—so wide
it took three whole days to walk across

And Jonah walked right in
walking one day's worth into it
then cried out, saying
just forty days more
and Nineveh falls

And the people of Nineveh believed the Lord
they cried out, calling for a fast
then all of them dressed in sackcloth
from the greatest on down
to the smallest

And God's word reached the King of Nineveh
and he rose from his throne
removed his robes
covered himself in sackcloth
and sat down in ashes

And it was shouted throughout Nineveh
as the word of the king
and all his great men, saying
of man or beast
of flock or herd
none shall taste food or graze
none will feed, none drink water

They will cover themselves in sackcloth
the man and the beast
crying out to the Lord
with all his might—
and will not bear injustice

And each will turn away
from his hardhearted way
from the grip of illusion
that frees his hands from violence only—
who knows, the god may turn
and repent
and turn from his burning wrath
and kindly spare us our death

And the Lord saw
what they had made of themselves
how they turned from their bitter ways

and the Lord repented from the bitterness he said
that they would bear
he didn't make them bear it.

Chapter 4

And this appeared like a bitter justice to Jonah
a great bitterness grew inside him
it hurt him deeply

And he prayed to the Lord, saying
Oh Lord, wasn't this the exact word and vision
I had always delivered and known you by
when I was still in my own country?
this is exactly why
I wanted to leave your presence
for Tarshish, before you would call me
a second time
because I knew you as a gracious God
compassionate, long-suffering
and of great kindness
and would repent bitterness

Now, Lord, take my soul from me
for me it is a good thing to be dead
and leave the presence of the living
and the Lord said
can it be a good thing
that you are hurt so deeply?

And Jonah left the city
walking all the way through it
and beyond it on the other side
where he sat down, east of Nineveh
having made a *sukkah* for himself in the desert
to sit in the shade, in the fragile booth
until what is made of the city
is revealed

And the Lord God had provided
a castor-oil plant, making it grow large
up over Jonah's head, a cooling shadow
to save him from bitterness
to soothe him

And Jonah began to feel happy
with the castor-oil plant

a great happiness came over him
changing his mood

And the Lord had provided
a worm in the night
and by the time darkness had risen away
it attacked the castor-oil plant
which wilted, was already dry

And then, the sun already shining
the Lord had provided a desert east wind
blistering
and the sun grew fierce, attacking
Jonah's head, he was falling
into a daze, wishing he was dead
already, saying
for me it is a good thing to be dead

And the Lord said to Jonah
can it be a good thing
that you are hurt so deeply
and because the castor-oil plant
no longer can soothe you?
and Jonah was saying
it is a good thing to be hurt deeply
until I am dead like it

And the Lord said: *you*
may feel compassion, may identify
with the castor-oil plant
for which you did not labor
to bring here, did not provide for its growing
into a great plant—a sudden child of a night
yet in one night it was gone

And may I not feel compassion
for Nineveh, the great city
which has grown up here with more than
a hundred and twenty thousand men and women
all of them innocent of knowing
the difference between right (the hand that provides)
and left—and likewise
many, many animals?

ARCHAEOLOGIST OF DAWN
(The Book of Isaiah)

Open up and speak from the heart
a voice rushing through you
startling the air

a lover
rushing to the side
of a wounded mate

wind opening the door
of a deserted mountain cabin
a wounded mountain ram

lift your voice
like a horn
to your lips

calling to my people
they are guilty
they are wounded

hiding their wounds
inflicted on each other
within   in pride

indifference and self-righteousness
shout it openly   jar the doors and windows
of this House of Israel

because they're still looking for me
daily   finding pride
in looking like they're searching

all dressed up
in clothes of righteousness
like a moral nation

wearing the moral law on their sleeve
and acting
as if their integrity depends on it

as if they're beyond acting
so may approach me
like a judge over their house

asking for direction
in the immoral streets
anxious for approval of their way

anxious children
impatient to please
tugging at the sleeve of justice

why are we fasting a day
if you won't take a moment
to notice they ask

why are we humbling ourselves
dressed in mourning
sacrificing body

baring soul
if you won't know it
answer us

here it is
you ask for answered prayers
when you won't stop to think

thinking with your feet
carrying you to the marketplace
only of yourself

how to further your business
on the shoulders
of others

thinking with your stomach
the day you're fasting
an empty stomach-mind

unable to get past yourself
pushing and shoving
unable to stand still inside . . .

you fast with a vengeance
pushing past the inner voice
too bruised to rise and be heard

is this a day for rising
standing in my presence
expecting a reward

for physical sacrifice   for your fasting
bowing heads like royal footmen
like rows of bulrushes

parting for the heavy prow of ritual
self-serving ghost ship
with its real cargo of slaves

instead of your soul you save
face by fasting
and I can't see through *that*?

wake up to a day
beyond acting
for yourself

the Lord's voice speaks
for itself:
act for others

not with faces but hands
opening
locks of injustice

sophisticated knots
tied mentally and physically
around the poor and powerless

like a harness
to break their spirit
free them   break the locks

cut the reins of oppression
rise to the occasion
fast to free man's spirit

make a day for opening
your cupboards
sharing with the poor

open your house your heart
to the homeless
open your eyes

instead of filling your stomach
instead of harnessing the weak for it
look at the hopeless around you

put your hand through that invisible curtain
and throw a coat around their shoulders
those are men and women

flesh like you   desperate and blind
outside the walls you've built to hide in—
the *otherness* you reach for is *there*

all around you
nakedly human
to a soul undressed by kindness

bare hands
untying the cloak of self-serving pride
and wrapping it around a naked body

and then all around you
as sudden as light
to eyes opening in the morning

the light inside you breaks open
as certain and irrevocable
as dawn

you will see yourself
healed by a human warmth
in the reality of daylight

a sky clearing over you
like new flesh over a wound
your body will be whole

and you will see it in the light
of others   revealed
in care for the hurt you've left behind

and openness to those you find
on the way of your future
like lost memories of your creator

memory repressed
oppressed   dispossessed
now yours from which to speak

sing out openly
and the Lord returns
your voice

call into empty space
for help
and he answers "Here I am"

and if you open
the locks of injustice around you
rip open the curtain of suspicion

remove the ring from the finger of status
you point at the poor
and open your mind to them

removing the insults from your tongue
and if you open your hand
dropping your body's show of pride

showing compassion sharing your gift of life
pouring the milk of your kindness
for the starved and hopeless

then the light inside you
will rise like the sun
from the dead of night

and the depression hidden within you
will walk out openly   a child
free under an afternoon sky

the Lord will be behind you
always around you
water in the desert of your need

meat and strength for your bones
and over you gentle rains
your life a fruitful garden

a mountain spring
always running
under a clear sky

and many from among you will walk out
to build on your ruins
firming the shaken doors and windows

reaffirming the ancient foundations
of your ancestors
on earth

and you will walk out
in the universe
deep in the firmament

building from the ruins
of planetary bodies
renewing the foundation

of the changing universe
continually
by your presence

water of your body
unchanging air
of your soul

you will be spoken of
openly and everywhere
as discoverer of lost ways

restorer of faded memories
nurse to broken dreams
surveyor of a universal highway

landscaper of sand-swept paths irrigator of deserts
plasterer of broken walls rebuilder of broken defenses
archaeologist of dawn

making a world
to live in   secure
in the infinite light of reality.

(Chapter 58)

A CLOAK OF PRIDE
SLID FROM MY SHOULDERS
(The Book of Job)

Today again
my speech my poem
this hard-talking blues

this heavy hand
from the long deep writing
of my spirit

O if I could know
where to go
and there

find him
at home
in his seat of justice

I'd sit down there
to lay out my case
before him

my mouth would be full
like a river
of what my heart must say

my mind open
like a window
to hear his words

as easy to understand
as the sounds of people
on the street

I wouldn't be blown away
overpowered
by them

but my own voice would be steadied
like a tree outside
in a bracing March wind

wind between the wood
earthly music
stirring my spirit

in his house
where an upright open man
isn't afraid to confront him

to listen to respond
to contend   a human music
creating the air

for a higher justice
in which to hear
I'm set free

but now I look to the east
and he isn't there
west and a vast empty ocean

face north
like a true compass
see nothing

turn south
and he's still invisible
hidden from my ear

but he follows each step I take
even when I'm sitting doing nothing
and he puts me in the crucible

to have his gold
because I've walked all my life
toward his light

past the neon temptation
of unreal cities
surreal commercials for "normality"

my lips have opened
for his infinite word
in meditation

I've opened his book
in my heart
and read with open eyes

he is one
determined within himself
as end

and has an end
all changes all choices
rest in his mind

but how can I change his mind
his soul desires
and it's already been done

ancient history
past changing
beyond our time

here he hands me
part of a sentence
already out of his mouth

and there's more to say
just as the past fills
with more to discover

it makes me shiver
to think
I must face him

here on this earth
now in this life
present in the infinite

transfigured
as my inaccessible inner self
rises to his hand

I turn white
cold sweat of fear
washes across my face

I want to turn back
as if I'm walking in my sleep
out of a world I know

my own shadow
smiles back at me
a shadow in the night

the past is drunk with strangeness
and his presence
drowns my heart in naked space

because he brought me out here
into the darkness
where I must continue speaking

into the open
like a child holding tight
to the side of his trembling crib.

(Chapter 23)

Who can turn me around
until I find myself
back in the old days

the good days
God watching over me
the sun shining

inside me
like inner light
to usher me past the nightmares

on the screen of giddy youth
my life was in focus
around me   it was autumn

wife and children growing
my walks were bathed in light
in cream

the heaviest rocks in my way
smoothed out
like oil

I was as if transported
wherever I went
on a stream of affection

when I went out the city gates
or when I came to my place
in the city square

the younger men quickly stepped
aside   like a wave disappearing
while the older men rose to their feet

celebrities stopped
in the middle of what they were saying
and almost covered their mouths

the voices of politicians trailed off
like old newspapers
blown in the wind

their tongues dried up
dusty leaves
swept to the back of their mouths

I mean men listened to me
you could hear a leaf drop
they wanted my opinion

when I finished I was allowed
the clarity of silence
my words fell gently on them

like spring rain
they were attentive as trees
opening their arms

stretching their hands out gladly
as if their minds were open
to the sky

and when I laughed or
made light of things
they were almost stunned

to be reminded I was human
their eyes would light up
blossoms the sun smiled on

I directed their thoughts
to the best way   a revelation
they followed like actors visibly

in the presence of a master
a man who'd paid more than his dues
inspiring confidence in the disillusioned

their ears would open
and mouths speak of me
graciously

anyone seeing me
became a witness
to my openness

I embraced a poor man
and an orphan
and a man with no one in the world

to turn to
a man dying gave me a blessing
a widow smiled with joy for me

I opened myself
and a cloak of pride
slid from my shoulders

I embraced a sense of justice
that wrapped itself around me
like a warm coat in winter

I was eyes to the blind
and feet
to the lame

a father to the homeless
a light in the midnight window
to the stranger far from home

I was a destroyer of nightmares
like a gentle counselor
in an orphanage

then I said to myself
I will die
in the open arms of a family

and my seed in that nest
outgrow the arithmetic of a lifetime
the calculations of a mind

or historical lineage
my spirit extends beyond time
like a phoenix rising

from ashes
an ancient poem
from the dust of pages

my roots reaching out
for water
each new coming spring

and the dew shall lie all night
on my branches
and I feel the sweetness of that weight

on me
that miraculous touch
of heaven

waking my heart
made light again
by the fire of love within

my pen returning to the page
like an arrow to the heart
a love as strong as death.

(Chapter 29)

נחמיה

NEHEMIAH

SUKKOT

AN UNGUARDED JOY
   (The Book of Nehemiah)

RAIN HAS FALLEN ON THE HISTORY BOOKS
   (The Book of Ecclesiastes)

I.

The major festival of the ancient Jewish kingdom was Sukkot. It was known then as simply "The Festival," since none of the others were comparably celebrated. It was the fall harvest festival, as well as the inaugurating festival of Solomon's Temple; its significance touched all aspects of Jewish life. Its association with the land, and with Temple and nation, gave rise to its identification with Israel's independence—it was the great Jewish festival of independence.

After the First Temple's destruction and the nation's captivity, Sukkot went through a transformation. Later, following the return from Babylon, Sukkot was blended into the freshly reinterpreted calendar of Jewish observance. Passover may have become the dominant festival; still, the one in spring, the other in fall mirrored each other in popularity. Shavuot, the other major festival of ancient Israel, was never as widely observed. These festivals were described in the Torah, and the biblical significance of each was enhanced in Second Temple days. The beginning of this process is described in "An Unguarded Joy,"a passage from the historical Book of Nehemiah, as it connects the joyous celebration of the festival to the biblical symbolism of the *sukkot.*

Sukkot, the plural of *sukkah*, are fragile booths. They became imbued with symbolism associated with the temporary dwellings in which the Jews lived during their forty years of sojourn in the desert, on their pilgrimage to the land of Israel. When the Jews had grown independent in both land and spirit, these booths could be remembered joyously, fulfilling words of the Torah. Thus, the *sukkah*, in some psalms and elsewhere in the Hebrew Bible, is used—in symbolic contrast to its actual fragility—as a metaphor for protection and peace, confirming its spirituality.

While this festival is one of joy in being promised a real home in the land of Israel, the tradition of festive rejoicing stems from the actual fulfillment of that promise in, first, the ancient kingdoms of Israel, and then the Second Commonwealth. The religious anchoring of this festival, after the Roman devastation, placed it in the biblical realm of Passover, which represented redemption from slavery, and Shavuot, which represented the revelation at

Sinai. Similarly, Sukkot represented the third step, after deliverance and revelation: the building of a home. In addition, Sukkot confronts the difficulty of living in an unredeemed world. Therefore, following loss of the home that had been built, the sweetness of Sukkot was tempered. Likewise, rituals became remembrances of Temple and national independence, though in a highly spiritualized way.

The early rabbis assigned the reading of Ecclesiastes to this festival, bringing to Sukkot the echo of Solomon's authorship (King Solomon, who inaugurated the first Temple at Sukkot) but also severe criticism of superstition, dogma, and belief in inflexible absolutes. Further, Ecclesiastes celebrates the joy of independence, yet at this point it is the independence and integrity of the individual.

Rabbis of the Middle Ages amplified the relevance of Sukkot by making the last day Simhat Torah (joy in the Torah). This revivified a "ninth day" of Sukkot, the extra day observed in the Diaspora. In the institution of a yearly cycle of Torah reading in synagogues, more closely binding the festivals to their biblical inspiration, the last book (Deuteronomy) is completed during Sukkot. Specifically, on Simhat Torah the last chapters, describing Moses' sighting of Israel from the Jordan and then his death, recall the vivid reality of forty years of wandering in the desert, as well as the symbolism of living in *sukkot*: joy tinged with the reality of having completed another year of reading the Torah reigns supreme, hence dancing in the synagogue takes over. Children (who on this additional day of Sukkot were included in the honor of being called to read the Torah scroll) may parade around the synagogue with flags, apples impaled on their staffs, echoing both independence and the beginning of the harvest.

Finally, the harvest season in Israel is followed by winter rains, so the end of the agricultural season parallels the end of the yearly Torah reading cycle and the beginning of the new. Following on the heels of the Days of Awe, Sukkot leads us into the seasonal reality of the festival year. An important element in the Sukkot liturgy refers to the ancient prayers in honor of rain, a theme I've echoed in titling my selections from Ecclesiastes. And in "An Unguarded Joy," a selection from the Book of Nehemiah, I've focused on the biblical authenticity of Sukkot.

II.

The Book of Nehemiah was edited in the fourth century BCE, though the history to which it is witness took place in the fifth century BCE, near the beginning of Israel's return from Babylonian exile. By this time, most Israelites were speaking Aramaic, the tongue spoken in Babylon and the lingua franca of the Middle East. The majority of people did not easily understand the Hebrew of the Torah, so translations into Aramaic were required. These free, paraphrastic translations were delivered by Levite interpreters in the earliest synagogues. "An Unguarded Joy" lovingly depicts this process.

Ezra read aloud the description of Sukkot in the Torah, which the majority of Israelites have forgotten. It was not likely that the common man studied the Torah in ancient Israel, so this passage describes the roots of democratization for Bible study, which culminate in the widespread study popularized by the Pharisees during Second Temple days. Sukkot rituals were similarly popularized; materials with which the festival *sukkot* were built and decorated in Israel are used to this day, not only in the *sukkot* themselves but symbolically in the synagogue ritual: *lulavim,* made of the prescribed tree branches, and the *esrog,* an indigenous fruit, are the main items.

The Book of Ecclesiastes (Kohelet in Hebrew) was edited (in the version we now have) during the third century BCE. Following biblical convention, the author speaks in the persona of King Solomon, who represents the source for the Jewish tradition of wisdom literature. The poetic wisdom of Ecclesiastes—much of it quoted from writings earlier than the third century BCE and perhaps originating in Solomon's day—is compiled in a way that suggests its final author was familiar with Greek philosophy. Greek traditions were then dominant in the Mediterranean, and beginning to cast their spell on educated Jews. There is also a residue of Babylonian cynicism in Ecclesiastes, but it is transformed, along with Greek stoicism, into a thoroughly Jewish and life-affirming mold, a monotheistic perspective. When Ecclesiastes was translated into Western languages, it began to sound too much like the worldly material it assimilated. As a result, to this day non-Jewish interpreters of the Bible mistakenly assume Ecclesiastes is a book full of corroding doubt. Doubt, yes, and quite sophisticated doubt, but the Jewish tradition was never one to suffer easy answers for very long.

I have attempted to restore a sense of the severe irony and poetic wordplay (especially in its biblical resonance) behind the sober tone of Ecclesiastes. Following so close on the Days of Awe, the reading of Ecclesiastes at Sukkot continues the process of self-analysis on a more worldly level. In its own time, the book complemented the critical side of Sukkot, which began in the books of the prophets. Prophets criticized the materialism and levity of "The Festival," and Ecclesiastes also casts a severe eye on spiritually debased values. Since Sukkot was a time when men were reaping their harvest and at their wealthiest, Ecclesiastes' scathing criticism paralleled the emphasis in the Book of Nehemiah on the ethical observance of Sukkot: the communal sharing in the festival, the giving of charity and remembrance of the desert trials. Much of the criticism seems aimed at the relatively wealthy and educated class, who were developing tastes for the worldly paganism of the great powers. The pagan modes contained heavy doses of fatalism and success-oriented goals, overriding the ethical values of Judaism.

Ecclesiastes is an intensely poetic book in the ebb and flow of its chapters, and I've made a free translation in contemporary idiom to counteract the distorted literalism of the usual translations. I've tried to parallel the Sukkot spirit described in "An Unguarded Joy" by offering a creative translation in the spirit of the biblical interpreters of Ezra's day, beginning the tradition of idiomatic Aramaic targums (paraphrastic translations). And the modern poets I've learned from, the latest instance being Robert Lowell in his translations from Aeschylus, parallel the Talmud's warning against slavish adherence to literalism.

What ultimately distinguishes Ecclesiastes from pagan traditions of wisdom literature is the ever-present sense of conscience anchored in biblical ethics. This Jewish underpinning softens the uncompromising surface tone and bathes the text in compassion—highlighted when Ecclesiastes is chanted in lilting tones on the second day of Sukkot, in the synagogue. When the book recommends the benefits of going to a house of mourning over a house of mirth, it is also celebrating the Jewish joy in an ethics of doing good works, fulfilling the spirit of the Torah.

AN UNGUARDED JOY

(The Book of Nehemiah)

Raised up on a platform
in full view of everyone
Ezra opened the book

he was standing above them
as everyone rose
when he opened the Torah

and Ezra made a benediction
to the Lord, God above all
and everyone answered amen

amen—with hands stretched to the sky
in a feeling of deep reverence
then bowed their heads

kneeling, until their faces
touched the ground
their lips to dust

and Yeshua, Bani, Shereviah
Yamin, Akkuv, Shabbetai
Hodiah, Maaseiah, Kelitah

Azariah, Yozavad, Hanan
Pelayah, and the Levites
they were the interpreters

so all would understand the tongue
of the Torah, and the people stood
in their places, listening

as the book was read and translated
slowly, distinctly, from morning till noon
with the sense made plain

to be felt and understood
the Lord's Torah
by all the men and women

then I, Nehemiah, as governor
and Ezra the scribe-priest and reader
and the Levites, interpreters to the people

said to them all
this day is a day made holy
to the Lord our God—be at peace

we must not mourn, we must not weep
because everyone was weeping as they listened
to the sweet words of Torah

then Ezra continued: go, celebrate
with a sumptuous meal, a sweet wine
and send a portion to those

who have nothing ready for themselves
for this is a holy day to the Lord
and not for being involved with ourselves

we must not look so burdened with grief
today sadness is forbidden
it is our happiness in the Lord

that gives us our very strength—
and the Levites also were calming the people
saying: calm yourselves, be still

this is a holy day
and not for carrying personal grief
today no sadness is allowed

then the people went home to celebrate
to eat and drink and
distribute portions for everyone

to make a great festival
in the spirit of shared happiness
an unguarded joy

because all had heard and understood
the words openly read to them
and felt their sweetness within

and on the second day
all the heads of families
the priests (Cohens) and teachers (Levis)

gathered before Ezra the scribe
to look more deeply
into the words of the Torah

and there in the Torah they found
written before their eyes
by the hand of Moses—

inspired by the Lord—
that the family of Israel will dwell
in *sukkot* (booths) during the festival

of this month—the Sukkot festival
and when they heard this, together they made
a declaration, to be read in all their cities

not only Jerusalem, saying
go to the mountainside
gather branches of olive and myrtle

leafy palm and boughs of willow
from which to make *sukkot*
as it is written

so the people went out of their cities and towns
to gather them and make the booths
each family made one on their roof

or in their courtyard
or in the courtyard of the Lord's House
in Jerusalem

and in the avenue leading
to the Water Gate, and the avenue
leading to the Ephraim Gate

the whole community that had returned
from exile, returned
to make festival *sukkot* and dwell within

and since this had not been done so lovingly
from the wilderness days of Joshua
to this day (or so it seemed)

there was a great happiness
a deep joy
in living the words they were hearing

and Ezra continued reading from the book
day by day, each festival day
continuing in the Lord's Torah for seven days

and on the eighth day (Shemini Atzeret)
they held a solemn assembly
a closing celebration—as it is written.

(8:5–18)

RAIN HAS FALLEN ON THE HISTORY BOOKS
(The Book of Ecclesiastes)

I.

You can't take it with you
a breath
all we take in

in a life of action
and exhaustive playback
breath into breath

what progress
what dumb thing can we make
under the sun

out of human hands
greater than our sweat, glistening
in the brief flash of a human life

generations rise and fall
to the earth
that hardly changes

the sun also rises
and falls, gliding
beneath us

back to its starting place
like wind always returning
to us—from any direction

rushing past us
turning and returning
all rivers run

to a body, a sea
that hardly changes
like our deepest thoughts

contained in history
and the seabed of instinct
our words exhaust us

we are speechless
before this flowing
our eyes and ears

forever look and hear
and that's all they know
perfect little machines

everything that happens
happened
happens again

there is nothing new
to grow wild about
under the sun

including the man wildly shouting
"Look, this is new!"
he lived ages ago

in the beginning of time
before records
and even tomorrow

with its memory machines
is lost in space
by the men approaching the end.

II.   (1:12)

I, the poet
was a king
in Jerusalem

I opened my mind
to explore to feel
everything

every reflection
under the sun:
an overpowering work

God gave a man
to make
with his life

I saw everything happening
under the sun
you can't take it with you

you breathe out
and a little wind shakes the world
alive around you

you can go with the wind
until you're exhausted
or against it and blue-faced

you can't save your breath
and you can't take
what isn't there

a tree bends to the sun
we can't straighten it
our mind can't overpower it

I said in my mind
I've grown rich
on experience

I'm the richest man
in Jerusalem
but what is this mind

and this desire
to abandon ourselves
in front of it

and I almost went mad
trying to add up
what I had

I grew nervous
I couldn't think straight
I was lost in the sun . . .

it's painful to hold
everything you own
inside

we can't take it—
rooted
to the air.

III.　(2:1)

I said in my mind
I will abandon myself
take life as it comes

but that is another mirage
the laugh is on the escapee
as life passes him by

I made this experiment
drink and smoke a lot
embrace pleasure

but meanwhile: keep my purpose clear
and open to insight
think: what's best

for a brief little life,
thinking or feeling?
so I set to work

in the grand style
building an *oeuvre*
ten books in five years

works of love and despair
naked and shameless
I was married and divorced

I went to all the parties
the glittering eyes
and wit: passion-starved

a trail of blinding jewels
of experience behind me
more than any king in Jerusalem

I tried on every life-style
I pushed to the center
through many gaudy affairs

I was surrounded by stars
singers and dancers
and fresh young bodies

to choose among
at the slightest whim
I was high and I was courted

but I kept my sense of purpose
every imaginable distraction
surrounded me

I opened myself to sheer
luxury of feeling
my mind was out there

on the windy ledge
and this is what I learned:
we can take in *anything*

and we are still empty
on the shore of the life
our blood flows to.

IV.   (3:16)

But when I looked further
under the sun I found
sitting in the seat of justice

beasts
and in the lap of wisdom
lizards

I heard myself thinking
the creator has made a road
from the heights of wisdom

to the conscience in every man
and each must find his way
meanwhile the court is abandoned

to the claws of influence
the school is abandoned
to the gnawing animal of despair

a season of disbelief
blows sand in the eyes
of the Lord's creatures

and I saw clearly
men are not higher than the camels
they must ride on

horse and rider
both arrive together
at the end of the journey

their skeletons come clear
like maps to nowhere
buried underground

their bones gallop into dust
together   they both run out
of breath

a breath is all
a creature takes in
in a lifetime of action

it joins the infinite grains of sand
on the shore of the life
its blood flowed to

who knows if the man's spirit
rises
while his faithful steed's falls

who has seen this parting of ways
in the midst of his own journey
fixed in life's precious saddle

and so I came to see
man is made to be happy
taking care and keeping clear

his own vision
embracing the world
with the arms of his work

along the road
of his conscience
who or what

manner of creature or act
could bring him far enough
out of himself

out of the sun's pull
to see the unbreathing future
beyond the living present

and beyond the little picture show
of stars and galaxies
cheapened by superstition.

V.   (4:1)

Then I returned
to consider again
the oppression constant as daylight

returning under the sun
here are the cisterns of tears
of all men oppressed

by the ravenous animal
of injustice   no one human
enough to offer an arm

and shoulder of consolation
here are the fists of power
in sleeves of comforting armor

the dead are better off
having found some consolation
more than the living

still trembling inside
before a concealed weapon
death

and better off than all
the unborn   uncalled
to being witness

to the heavy work
of men holding down
men

drowning each other in air
absorbing the power and
dimming the light

in the bloodstream
under a sky
made of skin

human energy I noted again
comes from a heart's
envy of the world

it sees itself in mind's mirror
as a galley slave   its horror
gives birth to "free" enterprise

so, concealed beneath the surface of excellence
and talent and plain hard work
is a motor of fear

running against each man's neighbor
and the fuel
is suppressed desire

pressure to be free of the power
of others   and so
breathing itself becomes a mechanism

empty of spirit
men are busily at work
building models of this

the race is on
to the heart
of the human machine

and men are proud of this ladder of "progress"
of where they stand
in the eyes of status (their neighbor)

then there is the man who is
his own totem:
a brain made out of wood

hands glued together with indifference
to the rat race
thinned by idiocy instead of tension

so which do you prefer
a vain idiot or an idiot vanity
how about a breath of fresh air

instead of rigorous incense!
a handful of quietness
instead of both hands shaking at the grind wheel

and the heavy perfumes of oil and sweat . . .
then I looked away and saw more
futility masquerading under the sun

the man or woman determined to be alone
no one beside them
no family no children

so why are they working so hard
salting away money and power
piling up credit promiscuously

around the clock
no time to even think
just who am I sacrificing

my time my pleasure for
who am I and who will know me
when I'm gone

the apple of this one's eye
is gilded to conceal
a core of depression

but just as oppressive the clichés
like two heads are better than one
sure: they cover each other's failings

if one of them falls
the other can lift him up
yes there's brilliant logic in this!

for how foolish one looks when he sprawls
having fallen all alone
without the grace of even someone's worried look!

also two who are sleeping together
get some warmth on cold nights
one alone gets only cold   and looks ridiculous

and is exposed to attack
while two link together
and with another make a chain   to brandish

or a coat of mail
yes friend- and kinship
is a power that binds

like word to word an oath (however false)
to keep or hurl with confidence—
but one all alone is blown in the wind.

VI.   (4:13)

They say it's better to be poor
when young—and wise
than a rich, old celebrity

a king   clamped
in the throne of his mind
unable to hear the clamoring streets . . .

the youth can walk freely
out of a king's prison
to become a king himself

while the born leader
even become a dictator
can only topple over

in his heavy mental armor
reduced to his knees
like a wordless beggar

but then I thought about that youth
rising to take his place
how the mass of people were inspired

by him   by his success
as people embrace the rags-
to-riches morality play

the longing masses
eager to start over
to wipe the messy history slate clean

and suddenly the man as all men
is gone   and his son
slouches in his place

rain has fallen on the history books
and the sun bleached it dry
for the new generations

which are endless in number
as were the ones preceding him
and for both alike he is unknown

the living page of his time
bled white out of memory
another page lost in the sea of the present

where even the beautiful craft
of inspired imagination
have their sails reduced to tatters

and their vain hopes discolored
like old photos
by the vague tears of sentiment

the memory of that star
like any moment of triumph or despair
is cut loose from the mooring of its time

adrift like a lifeless raft
after an explosion
after the countless explosions of moments

and the photos a living mind has made
in fits of hope or doubt
forgotten utterly as the sounds

of shutters clicking open
spoken words
a wind has blown away.

VII.   (6:1)

Another thing I see
weighing men down
in the invisible backpack

harnessed to every walker in the sun
or at the feet of one freely standing
is the load of injustice

a man or woman shining
in the eyes of their community
standing tall in mirrors of themselves

sure of their identity in the stylish dress
of God-given talents
confident on red carpets of success

rolled out from houses that hold
everything you could wish for
a happy family and nothing to wish for

a spirit filled to the brim
a table spread before him
but then— he can't eat:

he hasn't been allowed an heir
a visible future
as the present eats away inside him

someone else embodies his desire
his appetite materializes as another man
real or imagined

his fortune feeds that person
a stranger in the lap
of his reality

he stands before an empty mirror
staring into the abyss of vanity
unforeseen

(some other man will absently lounge
in the warmth and care
he skilled his hands to open)

and even if he were surrounded
with a hundred sons and daughters
and lived to a ripe old age

happiness could elude him a hundred ways
like echoes bouncing off stone
in a desert canyon

echoes from one unguarded shriek of recognition
terror-flash of the material world
black glimpse of an eternity

a nightmare instead of a miracle
a nuclear bomb
instead of a warming sun

all in a moment stripped bare by frustration
his soul stripped like a woman
in the midst of a crowded market that

was the world of his possessions
even if he were to live forever
that moment would gape behind him

like a freshly dug grave
the echo of violent recognition
and the vast explosive mirror-reality

of anti-matter   blind to his reflection
in a soul   irreducible
shaping the universe within   heaven and earth

but he can only see the face of horror
the hot flash of recognition: only the material evidence
a momentary picture but haunting him everywhere

a stillborn child   even a fetus
aborted is better off
than someone in the midst of everything

life has to offer and still restless
in the desert of awareness   blunt exposure
to a sense of happiness somewhere lost

like the innocent whiteness of skin
under a desperate tan
worse off than that embryo of darkness

innocent of the self-made light
of inner desperation   who comes
in passionate night sighs

and leaves before dawn
no one seeing its face
its name its sex bundled in darkness

better off not having breathed
or seeing its image inflated
in its own eyes

for it never had to bitterly wish
for a comforting darkness
to be gratified in

even if the man lived a thousand years
two thousand
what good is the sum of his breaths of air

if he's satisfied with nothing but a wish
with which to pay for his journey
to the same dust as all that have beginnings

this person's work kept his mouth full
and still he gasps for air
on the shore

what difference does it make
if it's Siberia or the Riviera
to a fish out of water

what good will books and travel
do us   wise man and fool
flop in the net of their longing

following the wind
our breath longs to catch
as if we could be somewhere else

and the realist making his way
in caution and poverty
thinks he should have been born rich

this makes bitterness "real" instead of "imagined"?
it's better to hold a bull by the horns
than have two in the bush?

what you see is what you get:
more bull   the eyes never stop
walking down that narrow aisle

of the universal supermarket
which is another illusion
like theories of objectivity

like the posters of mild Hawaii
we make what we see
with the eyes of a double

longing to be merely here
in our shoes
learning how to speak walk and be

more than a spectator
with the watery baby-eyes of an old man
just to be somebody somewhere anywhere: fully alive

this too is deadly illusion
just wanting to be
where we are already

pursuing the wind
that blows through us
as if we could be another.

VIII.   (7:1)

They say it's better to keep your name clean
than your body   whether bathing
in baby oil holy oil or covering a stink

with expensive deodorant
no man stinks more than a dead man
but, if left behind is the inner perfume

of a good name—then his deathday is happy
so no more false happy birthdays
until a man is dead

then he can be famous
without having to grease a palm or wear
the painted mask of success . . .

they say it's better to be with a family
burying their dead
than one celebrating successful occasions

for all will pass beyond
these forgotten fêtes
your vision will serve to remind them

you aren't eating your heart away
in feasts of gratitude or envy
but opening it

to the face of loss
all must wear
and all will remember your presence

they say the face of grief
is better than the laughing
party masks of plastic

the raw skin of sadness
though bad for one's complexion
reddens the blood strengthens the heart

and improves the mind
a wise heart is anchored
in a natural seriousness   at home

even at death with its wall of silence
even in a house that wails
in tune with hearts exposed and beating

while, running away from itself
a foolish heart capsizes
in a sea of nervous giggles

and flails desperately
behind a happy face of plastic
swimming back to its place at the party

under a paper moon
calmed by the stereo dutifully playing
"it's only a paper moon"

they say better listen to stinging
criticism from someone knowing
what they're talking about

than lending your ear to "friends"
you turn on like a radio
to the muzak of approval

the best tunes become idiotic
when translated for the mouse-eared
masses   inertia

is playing even more softly
under a muzak of desire
to be somewhere else

to escape into a soft sculpture
of the world created
and played on by heavies

having no idea what to do
with themselves   an empty talent
bottling air   milking respect

from wide-eyed calves looking
vainly for approval: the hot breath
in the nostrils of a bull

is what you get if not despair
served in silver trophy cups
empty as the occasions they honor

but even humility in the wisest person
allowing him to say
exactly what he sees

resisting influence and flattery
hardens into a statue of identity
to grace the social scene

"words to the wise" spoken at a cafe
like the coffee itself turns to oil
greasing the social mechanism

and he is also a helpless victim
of naïve hearts and eyes
he impresses his image upon

in his own naïve sexuality
mistaking love for innocence
gratitude for understanding

they say it's better to listen
to what you think
you have to say   inner ear

and eye open to what happens
to the event
in speaking in becoming a mirror a judge

everyone is hungry for images
of themselves   better see through that
than start up new fantasies

keep your conscience a clear window
to see through
as your death approaches from a distance

better a happy deathday
unsurpassed
than happy birthdays increasingly desperate

let what's there be
to feel smell hear see
before you gulp down something

like a hungry dog or baby
better to see a thing come clear
in the emulsion of time

than lose your integrity
in the rush of pride
to impose an image on the movie

to expose a frame too quickly
outside the nature time
of creation

don't get mad and impatient
restrain yourself
when everyone seems to be getting ahead

it's a stampede of mice
a rat race   madness
quickening the mass of Disney hearts

don't look back in anger
at boats you think you missed
or whine about good old days

while you frown in the idiot's mirror
reading wrinkles as ancient ciphers of a dilemma
central to the origin of the big cartoon

in the past most people are living in
the vast expanding bubble of "progress"
that suddenly bursts

throwing water in the face
of the philosopher on the beach
dreaming of fountains of youth

what depths of disappointment spring
from fantastic wells of expectation
sunk in the false bottom of fantasy land

don't be so dumb as even to inquire
in the studied falsetto of a scholar
where has the past gone?

it will smack you in the face
for having turned your head
at every passing fancy

of knowledge shaped by the girdle of progress
then there are those who study it
accumulating knowledge as if it were money

better to marry it
better yet inherit it
so there's time to sit in the shade

after gazing into the sun
its reflection off the metal
of coin

to sit in the cool shadow
of the mind's reflection   safe
in the reality of sun

the difference is
(between accumulating and having)
the wise man has a life within

a harbor for his ship to come in
illuminated by an inner reality
feeling the sun's power as light

falling around a field or page
not to possess it from towers
but letting it be revealed

observe this working of God
light   in its own time
as it reveals the touch of its creator

a tree bends to the sun
we can't straighten it
our mind can't overpower it

when a good day
comes your way
embrace it

and when the bad one arrives　watch out
but patience　observe the contrast
light creates a room for shadow

one creator made each day
so we don't build up expectation
as a wall

but may see the stones fall
names and reputations
material ripped away to an open view

of the present around us
the dimension of depth
sweeping between light and shadow

between inside and outside
the dynamic of waves
sweeping away the tower

climbed by the one thinking he was master
of what he could survey: past and future
but it is drowned

along with elaborate constructions of myth
fortune-telling and other dark fortresses
built for a false security

each day is constructed anew
in the flow of time　perfect as the sea
bearing a ship to its destiny

that is *felt* to be there
and in that feeling we can find no fault
with the nights and days that surprise us

in our beds of doubt or certainty
we are made perfectly awake
to the fathomless depth of creation.

IX.　(7:15)

I've seen everything
in the rich days I've walked through
like a long hall

in a home I thought I owned
and from life's windows
I've seen it all

though inside I had nothing
but a little wind
to keep my eyes from closing

I saw those who breathe deeply
in the rare atmosphere
of righteousness

and I saw them dying in it
from lack of oxygen
while cynics whose mouths are full

of lies grow strong and healthy
and live long lives
in their sewers of deceit

so don't climb up high
after perfection
don't get carried away

in the altitude of lucidity
nobody remembers who you are
when you fall on your face identityless

like a bright leaf blown by a wind
as strong and true
as a will driven beyond the imperfect body

but don't bend to natural forces
too easily   don't hold on
to the rail when the ship is sinking

don't cling to yourself like a child
to its toy
don't be a baby

still wailing inwardly
for attention   ruthless
don't stoop so low

to wear the wound of need on your arm
to play on the innocence of others
to be selfish as stone inside

the idol of yourself
why swallow a stone
the stone of bitterness you cast

and die before you've opened
a door to human kindness—
locked in the arms of deceit

squeezing the life away
of you and your victims   don't suffocate
don't be too self-involved

or selfless—hold on
but keep your mind open
let God anchor your conscience

freeing you to be
neither ego's slave nor wisdom's fool
you swim beyond the wreck

of single-minded arrogance
first one arm then the other
and a sense of a higher, deeper order . . .

on the one hand intelligence
is a stronger defense than
a pantheon of pious figureheads

there isn't a righteous cause on earth
without its empty-headed champions
promoting their own hot air

not one perfect man or woman
who is always right   uncompromised
by the slightest distortion in the mirror

by which he knows himself
and forgets himself too: the flaw
in taking memory for granted

a distorting memory   reflected
through the glass of
a highly compressed fear

for it will explode as sure as a star
just as the present is always erupting
dispersing the precious crockery of the past

into the lap of dozing Justice
who has forgotten this appointment
with the bill collector of Time. . . .

יהודית

JUDITH

HANUKKAH

WHO CAN DESPISE A PEOPLE WITH WOMEN LIKE THIS?
  (The Book of Judith)

I.

To understand why Hanukkah has become a more significant festival than orthodox tradition provided, we need an awareness of the Maccabean renaissance. The modern, Zionist renaissance created fresh parallels to the Judean state of 164 BCE–67 CE. A Jew in Israel today is familiar with many Maccabean sources, especially the First Book of Maccabees, in the Bible's Apocrypha. This is less true for Jews in the Diaspora, where watered-down retellings necessitate a healthy interest in modern histories of the classical Greek and Roman periods in order to understand the Maccabean age. Yet it is in the nature of Hanukkah to require study and insight into the classical roots of Western civilization, as well as into Jewish history and tradition.

So Hanukkah may now be the most sophisticated Jewish festival in its sources and inspiration. What is more difficult for a Diaspora Jew to grasp than the actual history, is the Jewish spirit and imagination of the times. Some of the imagination was assimilated from the dominant culture of the Mediterranean: the Greek—and Greek was a language used by educated Jews as well as some of the large Diaspora communities that existed at the time. Furthermore, as much as Purim, Hanukkah is a festival of special relevance to Diaspora Jews. The Jewish community of Alexandria, Egypt, produced the oldest surviving translation of the Bible, into Greek, underlining the biblical inspiration for Hanukkah: Maccabean descendants in the religious mainstream also continued to demystify the cultic use of the Torah, making it available to the masses.

Hanukkah itself created a renewal of ties between the Diaspora and Judea; in time, the festival revitalized the Jewish heritage and was observed throughout the Diaspora as a prooftext—as was Purim—of Jewish deliverance. In remembering the dedication (*hanukkah*) festival for the Second Temple (recovered in 164 BCE by the Maccabees from the Greek-Seleucid occupiers of Jerusalem), Hanukkah became a new link to the already ancient tradition. That first Hanukkah was celebrated like a "new Sukkot" (the festival that had inaugurated Solomon's Temple some eight centuries earlier).

As Sukkot was associated with Israel's independence, Hanukkah foreshadowed the renewal of the Jewish state. According to the Second Book of Maccabees (based on a historical record written less than fifty years after the first Hanukkah), the Maccabees had celebrated the Sukkot of 164 BCE in their hidden, wilderness caves. When they found themselves liberating Jerusalem, a few months later, a Sukkot-like inaugural of the Temple was appropriate. Yet this Hanukkah did not have the pomp and pageantry of Sukkot; the new Sukkot was a more domestic, personalized festival—which even boldly challenged some of the characteristics of pagan winter rites at that time.

In particular, Hellenistic torchlight processions and bonfires were radically countered with the Jewish ritual of lighting menorahs (lamps) in the Temple precincts. The inaugural lighting of the Temple Menorah was an important Sukkot rite, so it seems likely that a connection between the original Hanukkah menorahs and the Temple Menorah was part of the earliest Hanukkah. The Books of Maccabees imply as much, and the later Talmudic explanation of Hanukkah—the miracle of the lights (itself based on legends of hidden oil from the First Temple)—bear this out. The menorah symbolism further anchored Hanukkah in the Torah, connecting it with earlier dedications of the Tabernacle in Sinai, and then with the First and Second temples.

So the lighting of Hanukkah menorahs today is a remembrance of the Temple and the renewed Jewish state. But it is the imaginative transformation of the menorah symbolism which typifies Hanukkah spirit: the domestication, personalization and popularizing of traditional Jewish remembrance. By the time of Josephus (the Roman Jewish historian of the first century CE), Hanukkah was already known as the "Festival of Lights." The Hanukkah lights mark a resistance to the Hellenistic religion and culture, which was threatening to convert Judaism to its sophisticated idol worship and cult of selfhood. At its most telling, Judaism drew the line between the ethical construction of selfhood and the Hellenistic *worship* of it in pagan temples.

As with Purim, it would be a mistake to consider this festival as merely a commemoration of a historical event—Hanukkah grew and survived precisely because it was not. It confirmed that redemption was anchored in a continual test of imagination, interpretation, and faith in the immovable core of monotheistic vision. Hanukkah symbolizes the world-consciousness of Jewish culture and the maturation of a religion with universal relevance to human history.

The basis of the Hellenization of local cultures (as imposed by the Greek empire) was its appeal to universalism: it was open to all willing to give up their individual heritage (for the "betterment of mankind"). It would become the collective human culture, and even the *unwilling* would have to submit. The Greek-Seleucid Empire, and even some Hellenized Jews, fought the Maccabees and their descendants for more than a hundred years after the successful Jewish resistance. This we remember at Hanukkah. The Hellenic world could not tolerate the idea of a Jewish culture as deep and progressive as their own, or an independent Jewish state and religion. And the Maccabean revolution challenged the cosmopolitanism of Hellenized Jews, who assumed that the Jews could depend on benign "humanitarianism" for their rights. Finally, the Maccabean renaissance of Jewish faith challenged the Hellenized Greek religion, full of pagan idol worship in addition to mesmerizing rituals and sacrifices to pacify the masses.

We can see the same forces at work today, particularly among nominal Jews who trust in cosmopolitan clichés of humanitarianism. Do not the Moslem world and the communist world, like the fascist world and the Christian world, perceive a threat from Judaism? Jewish integrity tends to distort the universalist pretensions which cater to the masses.

For most Jews, Judaism means a way of living and acting based on ethical and spiritual standards. For the majority of the pious, this Jewish life is not easy, but still deeply gratifying. And the non-Orthodox Jew must define himself both in terms of the traditions and against the assimilating majority, who prefer the easier path of historical amnesia. Today, this may take the form of disbelief altogether, in favor of a surface "modernism" and "worldliness." So Hanukkah's relevance has been sustained through twenty-two centuries on a hard-won optimism that recognizes there are no easy, all-purpose solutions to the world's problems.

The determination of the Maccabees was based on vision and realism. That realism recognized the universal core of Judaism, and reached out to embrace even the most self-hating or assimilating. And the Maccabean renaissance was strong enough itself to assimilate much of the Hellenistic culture. Consequently, the roots of Judaism as a world religion—aware of its role in the world—flowered in this time. The first Hanukkah was anchored in the already ancient tradition of earlier "hanukkahs" (and to the events in Sinai via Sukkot, as well as the original Tabernacle), so it survived and grew in resonance after the Roman destruction of 70 CE.

Subsequently, rabbis of the new Diaspora began to interpret Hanukkah in traditional, religious terms, providing a poetic story full of ancient resonance: the miracle of the little cruse of oil. This story served to reunite Hanukkah with its Sukkot spirit of a joy tempered by realism. So, the Hanukkah menorahs, like the Temple Menorah during Sukkot, symbolize the future as well as the past: the unbreakable witness to the world that is Jewish integrity.

II.

The Maccabean renaissance produced books, movements, and ideas that were notable for being imaginatively based on tradition (though too pretentious to actually replace tradition, as in the additions to the Books of Daniel and of Esther, and the Books of Maccabees). The monotheistic focus of that tradition continued to produce works very different from any in the world. The Book of Judith was one of many Maccabean works that paralleled Greek romance in style but were deeper in dimension: a type of prophetic history tempered by an ethical sensitivity.

The Book of Judith is one of those works that tell the story of Hanukkah in an imaginative way: Jewish integrity resisting the mass movements of cultural and spiritual imperialism. The story of Jewish vulnerability and triumph in this book is a poetic parallel to the Maccabean struggle against vast foreign power. The Maccabean imagination in the book was true to the difficult, hard-won values in accord with which conscience required a spirit of resistance. In addition, education and imagination were valued in the service of truth, not power.

Preserved in the ancient Jewish translation of the Bible into Greek, but lost in the original Hebrew when it was relegated to the Apocrypha, the Book of Judith was probably read during the Hanukkah festival in late-Maccabean times. The poignant allusion to the rededication (*hanukkah*) of the Temple in Chapter 4 would not be lost on a Maccabean ear.

Jewish tradition preserved the story of Judith for Hanukkah in outline form, as in the medieval *Scroll of Antiochus*, but these later versions are pale imitations of the Maccabean imagination at work in the Book of Judith. More recently, the book has been retranslated into a Hebrew resembling the original. I have worked from a modern Hebrew version. Specifically, the Book of Judith is written in a highly poeticized form of narrative that loses its texture in a prose translation. For instance, one of the main poetic features is frequent use of biblical quotations, phrases, and parallels to deepen the rhythm and harmonics of the narrative. In fact, the narration is often secondary to the immediate feelings these echoes arouse. And there are the large sections of formal poetry themselves: psalms, prayers, songs, and invocations.

The final composer of the Book of Judith used legendary and historical material of much earlier date, just as the classical Greek dramatists used ancient mythic material. The story of Judith probably originated in Israel during the fifth century BCE, when the memory of the Jewish exile in Babylon was in the process of becoming archetypal: the same Nebuchadnezzar of the Book of Judith is met in the Book of Daniel, and both may be archetypes for the Greek-Seleucid Antiochus, of Maccabean times, in the eyes of the final Maccabean editors of those books. It would be unlikely that Maccabean authors were ignorant of Greek writing, though their Jewish orientation would toughen their resistance to its charms. For the Greek works of the time (and even the classics) were potent religious works, so that, in Jewish eyes, their spiritual and ethical sensitivity was crude.

In the *Agamemnon* of Aeschylus[1] (in the Robert Lowell translation of 1978), Clytemnestra, the queen, murders her husband—"I offer you Agamemnon,/ dead, the work of this right hand"—an act motivated by crude vengeance. "Oh, deceiving and decoying Agamemnon to my trap/ was work for a woman. I did the thinking"—the complete antithesis of Judith's selfless courage. And when the Book of Judith's author exaggerates mythic tradition, as when Judith invokes passages from Genesis that describe Dinah's youthful affair, righteously distorting them to justify the vengeance of Dinah's brother, Simon (conveniently ignoring their father, Jacob's, disapproval), there is still an ethical basis to Judith's prayer. Not so in the invocation of the massacre at Troy, by Aeschylus' Herald in *Agamemnon*, where no moral sensitivity is at work: "Their fields are scorched. Their houses are rubble./ Their seed has been wiped out from Asia. They were house-breakers, pirates and rapists." It was not a matter of realism in those days, but of moral focus: the Greek authors "modernized" the psychological depth of their heroes, while the Jewish authors modernized the heroic convention by fleshing out its monotheistic focus. The prototype for Judith was the pious "Woman of Valor," from the biblical Book of Proverbs. And the language and structure echoed the long tradition of great biblical books.

A passionate poetic narrative, the Book of Judith is motivated by intense outrage at the arrogance of pagan Greek imperialism. This rage is sublimated into the presentation of a beautiful woman who is Judaism itself: religious, but (at the same time) acutely oriented to reality. Her sublime physicality, rooted in domestic happiness and a sense of communal responsibility, contrasts with the inflated pride of the pagans. No angels or miracles are employed in this victory: justice is done when the enemy does *himself* in, a victim of his own arrogance. The victory celebration in the book is a literary antidote to the cruel intentions of the enemy. It is as obvious a conventional exaggeration as the victory over Haman, in the Book of Esther. Likewise, the popular imagery of war, heroism, and piety is highly stylized—the real passion in this poetic narrative lies elsewhere.

As in most Jewish writing, when vengeance is invoked, it is as a mirror image for the attacker's own self-destruction, a hope that he will be trapped by his own destructive plans. Judith's beauty was an instrument of truth allowing Holofernes and the inflated self-pride of the worldly power he represented to fall on its own face.

A reading of the Book of Ecclesiastes at Hannukah—in the Maccabean spirit of a free translation—might also be appropriate, since it is a model of the strength of Jewish tradition in resisting—and superseding—the Greco-Roman sense of its own cultural superiority. Significantly, the Book of Ecclesiastes is the biblical scroll assigned to Sukkot, Hanukkah's biblical root. But Hanukkah is the one festival that came too late for a scroll, though Judith was probably read in synagogues as a Hanukkah scroll during Maccabean times.

---

[1] Robert Lowell, *The Oresteia of Aeschylus* (New York: Farrar, Straus and Giroux, 1978).

(The Book of Judith)

In the twelfth year of Nebuchadnezzar's reign, he began to plan a war against the powerful nation of the Medes. When Nebuchadnezzar called on smaller nations to join him as allies, they refused—unafraid—sensing his power was overplayed. He was severely embarrassed, so that, when he later defeated the Medes, he planned retribution.

Holofernes, the Assyrian Army's commander in chief, put together a huge expeditionary force, with over a hundred and twenty thousand foot soldiers alone, and marched out of Nineveh toward Damascus, intent on destroying all resistance. The method was simple: wipe out local religions and cultures. After devastating various nations, leveling towns across Mesopotamia and Arabia, "butchering all who resisted," the Assyrian approaches Damascus.

*

And he surrounded the Arabs
burning their tents, looting their flocks
then came down into the plain of Damascus
it was during the wheat harvest and he set fire
to the crops, the fields were ablaze
herds destroyed, villages ransacked
and all the young men skewered on the sword

Panic gripped the coast
in Sidon, in Tyre
in Sur, Akko, Jamnia
Ashdod and Ashkelon lived in terror
they sent their highest messengers
begging peace: "We are here as servants
of the great Nebuchadnezzar, to lie at your feet
do with us what you like
the doors of our warehouses stand open
our flocks, our herds are under your command
every farm and field of wheat
lies at your feet
use them as you like

our cities and every citizen in them only wonder
what they can do for you, what's your pleasure"

these were their exact words to Holofernes
then he descended the coast and garrisoned the cities
where he made allies, chose conscripts
and received a hero's welcome
with garlands, tambourines, and dancing in celebration
meanwhile his army set fire to border villages
destroying claims to independent boundaries
he cut down all their groves of sacred trees
demolished all their pagan shrines
defiled every god they'd clung to
so it would be realistic for them to turn
to Nebuchadnezzar as a god
uniting nations under his worldly power
transcending all their local languages

Holofernes approached the valley of Jezreel near Dothan
where Judean mountains begin to be seen
he pitched camp between Geba and Beth Shean
staying there at least a month to regroup
and gather supplies for his army

By now the Jews in Judea had heard about Holofernes
commander in chief of the Assyrian army
under King Nebuchadnezzar, and how he dealt with nations
looting their sacred shrines, then leveling them
the Jews were quite scared, near despair for Jerusalem
place of their one God's temple
they had hardly returned from exile
only recently had rededicated the devastated Temple
cleaning the altar, restoring the vessels
reunited in their land.

(2:26–28; 3; 4:1–3)

*

Unlike the surrender pleas of their neighbors, the orders from
Jerusalem were to occupy the mountaintops and passages, buying
time for the protection of Jerusalem. The Jews were in no position
to defend their country militarily, but they could hope to appear not
worth the trouble of subduing. And they could pray for survival. It
wasn't a victory they prayed for, but to be spared a massacre and
cultural annihilation.

When Holofernes heard that Jews had closed the passages to Jerusalem, he was astonished. He asked his local allies what gave this people the nerve to resist, and he was told: faith in their God, demonstrated by a long history of survival. The Assyrian and his generals were furious when they heard this unrealistic answer, since Nebuchadnezzar obviously deserved to be recognized as the only god: his power and strength were visibly evident.

So Holofernes gave orders to wipe out this people. And the local allies advised a siege of the strategic city guarding the best route to Jerusalem. This way, the strategic mountain positions of the Jews would be useless and the Assyrians wouldn't lose a single soldier in battle.

After thirty-four days, Bethulia ran out of water. People were fainting in the streets. The town council accused its leaders of a grave error in not begging peace, like other peoples. They would rather be alive as slaves than watch their children die. As a last resort, one leader appealed for holding out five more days; if nothing changed by then, he would advise surrender.

Judith, beautiful and devout, a widow still in mourning, visited the leaders and accused them differently. Who were they to set a time limit for God? They were actually negating their faith by setting conditions for miracles.

But Judith declines to pray for rain when she is asked. When she does pray (in the psalm beginning Chapter 9), it is for strength and guidance in a plan of realistic action.

*

Then Judith kneeled
put her face in the dust
stripped to the sackcloth she wore underneath—
just at the moment the evening incense offering
wafted to the Temple ceiling in Jerusalem—
cupped her face in her hands
and spoke
her words rising outspoken
from her heart to the open sky
an offering, a prayer:

"Lord, God of my fathers
of Simon in whose hand you put a sword
to reward the strangers
who stripped off a young girl's dress to her shame

bared the innocence between her thighs
to her deep confusion
and forced into her womb
raped her in shock
to demean and disgrace her

"For you have said in the Torah
this is an outrage
and you allowed these violaters to be surprised
in their beds of deceit
the sheets stripped off them
their beds blushing with shame:
stained with their blood

"For the lords among these strangers
you allowed equal treatment with their slaves:
slain on their thrones
their servants in their arms
their wives and daughters allowed to be spared:
captured and dispersed

"Their possessions fell into the hands
of the sons you loved
for they listened to you
and were outraged
at the demeaning of a sister's blood
they called on you for help
and you listened
Lord, my Lord
now hear this widow's selfless words
you gave shape to the past
and beneath what is happening now
is your supportive hand
you have thought about the future
and those thoughts live as men and women

" 'Here we are!' they say
your thoughts are alive in the present
and you've cleared paths for them
into the future

"Look, here we are, exposed to the Assyrians
parading their well-oiled muscle
preening in the mirrors of their polished shields
bullying the hills with their herds of infantry

vanity worn on their sleeves: tin armor
their spears thrusting forward
their trust in their legs and horses
their pride in the naked tips of their arrows
their hope in thoughts of total domination—
so locked in the embrace of themselves
they can't know you are Lord over all
fierce in your shattering of wars themselves
great armies of the past are dust in your presence
they were lords in their own eyes as they marched on blindly
but there is only one 'Lord'

"Lord, crush their violence
break their thoughts to bits in your anger
at their shameless threats of power

"They want to force their way into your sanctuary
to cut off the ancient horn on your altar
to strip bare the ark
in which you are held holy
to demean your spirit with swords of tin and iron
to debase your name

"Look at the arrogance of their thoughts
cut them off in outrage
bow their heads in shame
sweep a mental sword through their minds

"Put your sword in the hand of a widow
give me the presence of mind
to overpower them with pointed speech
in the sheath of an alluring voice
to confuse them with an inner truth
shaping words of steel
to slay 'equally' masters with their slaves
servant and petty lord
while they are inflated by selfish desire
while they are charmed by feminine lips
while they are caught in their self-deception
shatter their pride
disperse their power
by a woman's hand
"Your force is not visible in numbers and armour
does not stand at attention before men of war
your power is indivisible and disarms violence

and you are a Lord to the powerless
help to the oppressed
support to the weak, refuge to the humble
a sudden rescue, a savior to the lost
warmth in the coldest despair
light in the most hopeless eyes

"Please hear me, God of my father
Lord of Israel's heritage
Master of the universe, Creator of earth and sky
King of all creation
hear my psalm

"Let my words be lies they cannot hear
sharpen my tongue with charm
my lips irresistible
mirroring their inner deceit
which stares back into their surprised faces
as my words cut deep
like a sudden knife
into those with cruel plans
against our heart, against your spirit
and the Temple of your spirit
the mountain of Zion
the house of your children
in Jerusalem, and let the whole nation
all nations
suddenly understand
that you are Lord and God and King
above all force and power

"And Israel stands
by your shield."

(Chapter 9)

*

Judith's prayer was over
she rose from the ground
called to her maid
and in the house removed the sackcloth
and widow's dress, then bathed
in creams and expensive perfumes
and did her hair
crowned with a subtle tiara
and put on her most attractive dress
not worn since her husband Manasseh died

and before that only on joyous occasions—
slender sandals adorned her feet
brightened by jeweled anklets
bracelets and rings on her arms and fingers
earrings and pins and other jewelry
making up such a beautiful picture
that any man or woman's head would turn—
she gave her maid flasks of oil and a skin of wine
fig cakes and dried fruit
a bag filled with barley cakes and roasted grains
cheeses
and loaves of sweetest challah
then carefully wrapped her own dishes
and koshered pottery
also for her maid to carry . . .

They kept walking straight across the valley
until sighted by Assyrian advance troops
who seized Judith, interrogated her
"Where do you come from?
What people do you belong to?
Where are you going?"
"I'm a daughter of Hebrews
but I'm escaping from them
because they are fodder for you
to be devoured as simply as grain in a bowl
I want to be taken to Holofernes your Lord
I can report the truth to him
I want to show him the simplest way
to take over the mountains and approaches
surrounding this country
without losing a single man
subduing it without so much as a bruise"

As these men listened to her well-chosen words
they saw the noble beauty in Judith's face
and (coupled with her directness) they were overwhelmed
by such physical elegance in a woman
"You have saved your life
not hesitating to come directly
into the presence of our lord
you will be taken straight to his tent
and we will announce you to him—
have no fear in your heart
when you are in his presence
because when you tell him what you told us

he will treat you with deep respect"
a detachment of a hundred men escorted the two women

So Judith and her maid came safely
to the tent of Holofernes—
but not without causing a stir in the whole camp
the news was buzzing from tent to tent
and while Judith waited outside the commander's tent
a crowd gathered around her
amazed at her beauty
this was the first they'd seen of an Israelite
and coupled with what they'd heard
they were amazed at the presence of this people
as their curiosity fed on her grace
"Who can despise a people with women like this?"
they were saying
"We'll have to wipe out this entire race
every last one of them
just as we were told to do
because any that survive will probably outwit
just about anyone in the world—
moved simply by the agony of loss
of such grace and beauty
to bring our world to its knees
as surely as a disarmed suitor"

Then Holofernes' personal guards came out
to escort Judith into the tent
where he was resting on his bed
under the fine gauze mosquito net
that was a precious, royal canopy
purple interwoven with fine strands of gold
studded with emeralds
and many other gems: as stunning as a crown

When Judith was announced he came out
silver lamps carried by servants leading the way
into the front part of the tent
and he saw her standing there and was amazed
at so beautiful a face
she bowed touching her face to the ground
in homage, but his servants quickly lifted her up
"Feel at ease, woman"
Holofernes was saying
"Have no fear in your heart

I've never hurt anyone who made the choice
to serve Nebuchadnezzar, king of this world
I didn't choose to raise a spear
against your people in the hills
they've brought me here themselves
insulting me by taking us lightly
now tell me why you've escaped from them
to join us—but first, be at ease
you have saved your life
take heart, you've found a new life here
free of fear
no one can threaten you tonight or any other night
you'll learn what it is to be at ease in your life
to be an equal and treated as well
as any servant of my lord, King Nebuchadnezzar. . . ."

*

Judith's speech before Holofernes, like other untranslated passages in the following portion, is inferred.

*

Judith's words enchanted Holofernes
they were so well-measured
all his attendants were amazed at such wisdom
"There isn't a woman in the whole world
to match this fresh intelligence
lighting up the beauty of her face"
And above the buzzing Holofernes said to her
"God has done well
to bring you in advance of his people
into our hands, strengthening us
so we may bring a just destruction
to those so blind as to take us lightly
having insulted my lord by refusing to kneel—
your God will right their wrongs himself
if you do as you've said
for your words are well chosen
and you are a beautiful woman
your God shall live and be treated as my god
as you will live in the palace
of King Nebuchadnezzar, so your fame
may spread through the whole world"

*

The fourth day after Judith arrived
Holofernes planned a private feast
bypassing the invitations most banquets require
to all the officers, and he called in Bagoas
his head eunuch who was taking charge of Judith
"Talk to the Hebrew woman
persuade her to join us for a feast
it's disgraceful not to know her better
everyone will laugh at us for not courting
such a beautiful woman while she's here"

When Bagoas came to Judith he was all flattery
"Have no fear fair lady
of my lord, and he will be honored
if you will come into his presence
to drink wine and be his guest
at an intimate feast
and be a chosen daughter of Assyria
beginning to live today
like a daughter in the House of Nebuchadnezzar"
Judith was ready with an answer
"And who am I to refuse my lord?
I desire only to be of service
pleasing him will make me happy today
and will always be
something I will cherish until the day I die"

And so she began to dress
in the fine clothes she had brought
in the cosmetics, jewelry and alluring perfume
and in gentle ceremony she sent her maid ahead
to lay the soft fleeces Bagoas lent to her
on the floor in Holofernes' tent
where she would eat and then lean back

When Judith came in and Holofernes saw her
leaning back on her fleeces
his heart was overwhelmed
and his mind filled with desire
lit by a wish to sleep with her
from the first time he saw her
in fact for these four days he'd been searching
for a way to seduce her

and so he was saying "Drink
relax and let yourself go with us"
"I'd love to, my lord
today I've found a reason to live
beyond anything I've dreamed of since I was born"

Facing him, Judith ate and drank
the food her maid had brought and prepared
and Holofernes having accepted her reason
for being true to her God's rituals
were disarmed at her acceptance of him
and so excited at the thought of having her
he drank to his heart's content
until he'd poured out more wine in one night
than he'd drank of anything in a day
since he was born

Now it was getting late and the staff
were leaving, tipsy, but quickly, as if they knew
Bagoas rolled down the outside tent flap
then dismissed the servants
(natural enough since they were exhausted)
and they went straight to sleep
leaving Judith alone with Holofernes
who had wound up sprawling on his bed
his head swimming in wine

Earlier, on the way to the feast
Judith asked her maid not to leave
if dismissed later, but to wait outside the bedroom
just as she did on previous mornings
since now everyone expected her early rising
and going out for ritual prayers
she had even reminded Bagoas and now
all had gone
not a soul important or unimportant
was left in the bedroom
Judith stood by Holofernes' bed
a silent prayer in her heart:

"Lord, my God, source of all power
have mercy on me for what my hands must do
for Jerusalem to be a living example
of trust in your covenant
now is the time to renew our heritage
give my plan life

to surpass the enemies
to bring them to their knees
who've risen up all around us
great herds coming to devour us"

Her hand reached up
for Holofernes' well-honed sword
hanging on the front bedpost
slung there in its jeweled scabbard
then, standing directly over him, swiftly
her left hand seized hold of his hair
"Make me steel, Lord, God of Israel—today"
as with all her strength she struck
at the nape of his neck, fiercely
and again—twice—and she pulled
his head from him
then rolled the severed body from the bed
and tore down the royal canopy
from the bedposts

A moment later she stepped out from the bedroom
and gave the head, wrapped in the canopy, to her maid
who put it in the sack she carried
with all of Judith's food and vessels

The two women walked out together
just as they usually did for prayer
they passed through the camp
walked straight across the valley
climbed the mountain to Bethulia
and approached the city gates.

(10:1–5, 11–23; 11:1–4, 20–23; 12:10–20; 13:1–10)

*

Chapter 14 and the beginning of Chapter 15 describe Judith's
reception in Bethulia, the rout of the Assyrians, and the victory
celebration. A subplot is concluded, in which Achior, a neighbor
who respected the Jews, identifies Holofernes' head, then asks to be
circumcized and is "incorporated in the House of Israel forever."
The book ends with the arrival in Jerusalem, followed by a brief
description of Judith's later life and death.

*

All the women of Israel come out to see her
on the way to Jerusalem

flushed with the victory they shared
of faith over power
grace and daring over brute force
some began a dance in celebration
Judith was carrying palm branches in her arms
passing them to the women around her
they were all garlanding themselves with olive
Judith at the head of the procession
to Jersualem, leading the women who were dancing

and the men of Israel who were following
dressed in their armor and garlands
songs and psalms from their lips
lightening the feet of the dancers

Then Judith began this psalm of thanksgiving
and all the people joined her, repeating the lines
the psalm of a Jewess echoed by Israel:

"Strike a beat for my God with tambourines
ringing cymbals lift a song to the Lord
a new psalm rise from a fresh page of history
inspired with his name
call on him for inspiration
My Lord is the God who crushes war
in the midst of the warmonger's camp

Jerusalem is pitched like a tent
in the camp of Israel
and here he has delivered me
from the grasping hands of my enemy

The Assyrian swarmed over the mountains in the north
with tens of thousands in armor
gleaming in purple and gold
hordes of infantry like rivers
flooding the valleys
an avalanche of horsemen
pouring down on the plains
my borders would be flames he said
my young men skewered on swords
infants flung to the ground
children seized for slaves
and my daughters for whores

But the Lord God has let them be outwitted
with a woman's hand

their hero fell
and not a young man's hand touched him
not the sons of warrior giants
neither a Goliath nor David
but Judith, daughter of Merari
stopped him in his tracks
paralyzed his brutal power
with the beauty of her face

And instead of fame for fleeting glamour
she is held in honor
because she didn't think of herself
but faced disaster head on
firmly on the open path, God's way

She put aside her widow's dress
to save the honor of the living
those oppressed in Israel
she anointed her face with perfume
bound her hair beneath a delicate headband
and put on attractive linen to lure him
but only to his own undoing
her slender sandal imprisoning his eye
her beauty taking his heart captive
for the sword to cut through his neck

Persians shivered at her boldness
and Medes shuddered in terror

My humble people were suddenly raising their voices
my weak little nation was shouting for joy
while the enemy, shocked, ran off in fear
they panicked as my people danced in the streets
the sons of mere women pierced their lines
mamas' boys chased them as they ran
willy-nilly they ran away like brave sons of eunuchs

Their battle lines were erased
like lines in the sand
under the pursuing boots of Israel

I will sing a new psalm to my God
Lord, you are great, you are our glory
your strength so marvelously deep, unconquerable
may all your creation recognize you
because you allowed everything here
to be

you said the word and we're here
and the breath behind it is our air
your spirit breathes the form of all things
it opens our ears
no one can resist your voice
the message of creation is always there

Mountains may fall into the sea
and seas crack open like a broken glass of water
rocks may melt like wax
but for those who live in awe of you
your presence is a steady candle
glowing warmth and a guide to safety
all the burning sacrifices are quickly mere fragrance
all the fat of sacrificial lambs a brief aroma
compared to one person in awe of you
whose strength is always there

All nations who come to destroy my people
beware of justice, you will disappear
your peoples will see a day of judgment
before God, My Lord
but all they will know is the fire in their hearts
sparked by inflated pride
a pain that will always burn there
as they are confined in the room of their minds:
their flesh will be consumed in it
and given to worms."

(15:12–14; 16:1–17)

אֶסְתֵּר

ESTHER

PURIM

A BANQUET OF DEDICATION
(The Book of Esther)

science. Dedicated to individual integrity, the Jewish world is based on a vision of history suffused with human purpose. It is not cleverness or foresight which saves the Jews, but dedication to their faith—unlike the whims of Ahasuerus and Haman, or the gullibility and self-interest of the masses, the actions of Mordecai and Esther are based in the service of God. The greatest contrast of all is revealed in the ascendancy to positions of power by Mordecai and Esther, who do not use this power for personal gain or social status, but to protect their simple right to live. In "The Banquet of Dedication," Ahasuerus asks Esther what she would have—up to half the kingdom. In the most poignant terms, Esther replies (her opening words sharply echoing the false humility of Haman): "and if your majesty pleases/ grant me my life/ it is my petition/ and my people's life/ it is my request—/ we wish to live."

The vulnerability of the Jewish Diaspora, as evident today as it's been for thousands of years, cannot be wished away. The vulnerability of Israel itself (as demonstrated in 1973) or the sudden change of fortune for contemporary Persian Jewry (in the Iran of 1980) are the latest reminders that the appropriate lesson of Purim lies in Mordecai's sense of preparedness when he counsels Esther not to reveal her Jewish identity. The joy and celebrations of the Jews in the Book of Esther are not for a victory, but for having maintained their sense of dedication to Jewish origins, allowing their enemy to be victimized by the same machinations of worldly power he wielded against Jews. So we get happily drunk—not on power, but in order to forget for a while the state of vulnerability that is sometimes a curse, though more often a blessing. It is no more a "chance" of fate that we read the Book of Esther today than it was mere chance to have survived in Esther's day.

As with the other festivals, Purim is rooted in the Torah. What is implicit in the Book of Esther is made explicit by the Talmudic commentators when they interpret the pedigree of Haman. The week before the festival of Purim, the portion read from the Torah (Chapter 25 of Deuteronomy) describes the treachery of the Amalekites and the necessity to remain vigilant, since their cruelty lives on in every age, symbolized in the genealogy of their descendants. In the Book of Esther, Haman is first described as a descendant of Agag, the king of the Amalekites, and we're not allowed to forget this, as the appellation is subtly repeated in later chapters. So the highly stylized end of Haman and his family is a literary response to the weakness of Saul's treatment of Agag (and his laxity in observing the injuction to remember the Amalekites).

The Book of Esther, like the Book of Judith, was probably edited in its final form near the Maccabean age, when there was a new tolerance for complexity of imaginative approach. All the stylistic sophistication of the Book of Esther would be lost on the ears of the Jews' enemies, who made a literal reading of it into an excuse for vilifying the Jews. During the "Age of Enlightenment," Martin Luther branded the Book of Esther as evidence of an immoral Jewish nationalism.

Finally, we remember Esther herself, whose natural beauty allowed her to serve her people. Esther's beauty was symbolic of the strength in Judaism: its spiritual and ethical roots, not its material power. Yet Esther (Hadassah was her Hebrew name) was at home in the courts of worldly power, demonstrating above all the expansion of Judaism into a universal religion and culture: not tied to local and cultic worship, like most pagan religions. The Book of Esther is an example of Jewish fondness for *this* world. There is no shame in Esther's beauty, nor is it gloried in, for she doesn't stand above her people in her queenship—on the contrary, she is presented in all her feelings as an ordinary Jewish woman. Though she is a "modern" woman at home in the world of 2,400 years ago, Esther's devotion to her Jewish heritage parallels that of the early pioneers in twentieth-century Israel.

The Jewish Greek translation of the Book of Esther, made in Egypt during Maccabean times, attempted to infuse it with a greater religious sobriety by putting prayers and poems in the mouths of Esther and Mordecai; these additions to Esther, like similar ones to the Book of Daniel, are part of the Bible's Apocrypha. The early rabbis rejected these additions, along with such other Maccabean works as Judith and the Books of Maccabees, because of their religious pretentiousness. Preserving the charm of the original Book of Esther allowed it to become extremely popular among youth, and the joy of Purim remains bright with the wide eyes of children.

The carnival masquerades of Purim, like the elements of satire in the Book of Esther, mask an underlying anxiety about Jewish vulnerability. In the same way, the joy of children at Purim and Hanukkah is the real face of these festivals—the anxiety of adults, with its overbearing and pretentious tendencies, remains in the background.

A BANQUET OF DEDICATION
(The Book of Esther)

Ahasuerus ruled a Persian empire of 127 provinces. He made a great festival for representatives from all of them, lasting half a year. Then he threw open the palace for the common people of the capital city, Shushan, for another seven days of feasting and drinking. Drunk and enraged by an imagined slight from Vashti, his queen, Ahasuerus heeds the suggestion of his councilors that she be deposed. The issuing of a decree, to be sent to all the provinces, cites this action as an example to all males of vigilant dominance. It is a rather comic decree, especially in its bureaucratic formulation, but the process sets the precedent for a later one, in which the prime minister, Haman, suggests the Jews be murdered. Both decrees blend a rational process and logic with a callousness bred by political power and the literal reveling in it.

A new queen must be chosen. Beautiful virgins from each of the provinces are brought to the capital. Esther, adopted daughter of Mordecai, is among the chosen. Both are fourth-generation, Diaspora Jews, dating from the Babylonian exile. Esther undergoes a twelve-month beauty treatment, as required in the king's harem, then is brought to the king and wins his favor. Mordecai, who remains close to her as an official in the palace government, has advised Esther not to reveal her Jewish origin. Subsequently, she is made queen. During Esther's coronation feast, Mordecai learns of a court plot on the king's life, tells it to Queen Esther, and so he, too, wins favor when the plotters are caught. The stage is set for Haman.

*

Not long after these things
King Ahasuerus appointed Haman
prime minister

so Haman, son of Hammedatha, the Amalekite
(remember the cruelty of Amalek)
was raised to the highest seat

among the high officials at court
and all the courtiers had to bow
right down to the ground for him

for this was the king's command
yet Mordecai didn't bow
let alone kneel to the ground

the officials at the King's Gate
asked Mordecai: how can you ignore
the king's commandment?

and this continued day after day
the courtiers reminding him
and he ignoring them

explaining that he was a Jew
words so striking and upright
these men exposed him to Haman

to see if Mordecai would stand
by his word
and be allowed to

and when Haman saw for himself
how he would not kneel
a rage swelled in him

that killing Mordecai could not satisfy
a deep contempt for this man's people
now that he was faced with them

until Haman could think only of how
to wipe out all Jews from his sight—
of whom Mordecai was one—

every last one
scattered across the vast kingdom
ruled by Ahasuerus

In the first month, Nisan
in the twelfth year of King Ahasuerus
they cast lots

or *purim*—as they were known
in the presence of Haman
who was looking for the day

of days, the month of months
which fell
in the twelfth month: Adar

There is a certain people
Haman was saying to Ahasuerus
scattered yet unassimilated

among the diverse nations of your empire
honoring different laws
from those of their hosts

refusing to honor
even the king's laws—
as long as they live

it demeans the king—
so if your majesty pleases
it would be in his best interest

and the state's
to issue a decree for their destruction
and expropriate all their assets

and I will raise several million in silver
for the king's treasury
to satisfy all involved

the king removed his ring
giving the royal signet
to Haman

son of Hammedatha
the Amalekite
the enemy of the Jews

the silver is yours to raise
the king was saying
and so the people are yours

if you please:
do what is right
in your eyes

Now in the first month, the thirteenth day—Passover eve
the king's scribes were assembled
and all that Haman ordered

was written down and addressed
to the king's ministers
to the governors of each province

and to the leaders of every people
each written in his own language
and each province in its own script

it was decreed in the name of King Ahasuerus
and it was sealed
with the king's ring

the letters were sent out
in the hands of couriers
to all the provinces, saying

the Jews must be destroyed
wiped out
you will round up the young with the old

little children with the women
and kill them
in one day of extermination

beginning on the thirteenth day
of the twelfth month
Adar

and everything they own
belongs to the executioner
loot it for yourselves

this document was to be published
as a decree—binding as law
in every single province

proclaimed in every tongue
so all would be ready
for the appointed day

the couriers left immediately
on this mission of state
even as the law was being posted

on the walls of the capital, Shushan
and Haman and the king
sat down to banquet

in the palace
but in the city of Shushan
tears and confusion reigned.

(Chapter 3)

*

When Mordecai learned of these things
he burst out in mourning
crying out, ceaselessly

dressed in black, in bitter grief
he walked out openly
in the midst of the city

in open protest
raising his voice inconsolably
a loud and bitter voice

a fierce protesting
right up to the King's Gate
a great mourning

as the Jews would make
in every province, loudly
throughout the entire empire.

(Chapter 4:1–3)

*

Esther learns of the decree from Mordecai, who asks her to
intercede with the king. But Esther, anxious and distraught, sends
word to him that she can't do it without breaking court protocol and
risking her life.

*

And when Mordecai heard Esther's plea
he did not hesitate to reply
returning her messenger immediately:

Esther, do not think for a moment
silently within yourself
that within the king's palace you are safer

than any other Jew
but if you persist in silence
in waiting

at a time so crucial as this
the Jews will still be delivered, yes
saved in another way, by another hand

but you and your family will pass away
like a moment of truth turned away from—
for you are only yourself for a reason

and who can know if you were not brought
splendidly into favor in the palace
for a moment like this—of action.

(Chapter 4:12–14)

＊

    Esther acts, expressing her solidarity with Jews by fasting with
them for three days. She risks her life, and it happens that her
weakened state from fasting inspires the king's generosity, who
grants Esther her petition. Before disclosing what it is, Esther sets
the stage by throwing a banquet of her own, to which Haman is also
invited.

    Meanwhile, Haman has already built a gallows to hang Mordecai
on. But before Haman can reveal Mordecai as a Jew, the king is
reminded of Mordecai's favor in having saved his life and orders
Haman to honor Mordecai by the same means that Haman had
devised for his *own* honor. So Haman has a foretaste of his
downfall—victimized by the quirks of chance in his own
plotting—before he arrives at the queen's banquet.

＊

And the king
and Haman came
to drink with Esther the queen

the king again said to Esther—
while they were drinking wine
on this second day of banqueting—

your petition is granted, Queen Esther
even if it means half the kingdom
your request will be fulfilled

and this time Esther responded
if I am worthy in your eyes
of the king's favor

and if your majesty pleases
grant me my life
it is my petition

and my people's life
it is my request—
we wish to live

for we have been sold
I and my people
to be slaughtered

murdered and destroyed
yet I would not have spoken
had I been sold merely

for a servant girl
and my people for slaves
I would not have troubled the king

with news of a plotter
whose hatred outweighs
his concern for your honor

Who is it? the king exclaimed
and speaking to Esther he said
who would dare turn his heart to this

and lay a hand on you—where is he?
An enemy, a plotter! she was saying
no other than this bitter Haman

as he sits before us
and Haman was dumb struck, confused
before the king and queen

and the king was so enraged
he stalked out from the banqueting
into the palace gardens

and Haman remained, trembling
but making a plea for himself
before Esther the queen

he had seen the king was convinced
and would make up his mind
to punish him

but suddenly the king returned
to the banquet hall
from the palace gardens—

Haman had fallen to his knees
and was now lying prostrate on the couch
where Esther sat

and the king was beside himself:
will he even violate the queen
rape her right here

while I am in the palace?
and the words were barely out
of the king's mouth

when it seemed the hood had already fallen
over Haman's face
like a man about to be hanged.

(Chapter 7:1–8)

*

In the concluding three chapters, the process of Jewish deliverance is presented in the most earthly, striking terms. Haman's
murderous contempt will be turned on himself and his family. The
end of the story remains as stylized as the beginning, so that we feel
the underlying Jewish ethic. It is not revenge the Jews exact of their
enemy, but the principle of *la'amad al naphsham*—the plotter
doing *himself* in.

It is not just Haman's end that must be resolved, but the whole
machinery of state and culture—which was set into motion, dis-
seminating racial prejudice—that has to be halted and reversed.
The real drama centers on the future of the Jews, not the fate of
Haman. As Haman's words remain an echo of anti-Semitic terror,
as Mordecai's and Esther's of fierce Jewish identity, so the major
theme of the Book of Esther emerges as one of redemption. The

Jews not only survived, but renewed their link with Jewish heritage.

So the final chapters, which unfold the true climax of the book, focus on the establishment of a new, great festival. We've witnessed the birth and joyous proclamation of Purim, a festival of deliverance and redemption, which becomes as deeply rooted in the Jewish year as Passover.

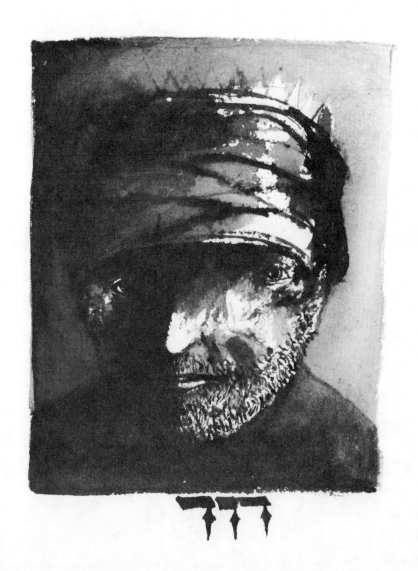

DAVID

PASSOVER

TO THE CHILDREN
(The Haggadah and The Talmud)

A FOUNTAIN FROM WILDERNESS STONE
(The Book of Psalms and The Haggadah)

ALL MY MEMORIES MELT INTO YOU
(The Song of Songs)

I.

Passover is probably the oldest Jewish festival, an illumination of the ancient covenant ethics of the patriarchs, which blossomed into the Pesach offering of free men. Passover became the festival of freedom—from slavery, from idolatry, and from superstitious fear. In remembering the process of Israel's birth as a people, the ancient revelation to mankind known as monotheism was also reenacted. By taking pleasure in following the Torah's instructions for observing the Exodus, joy in being Jewish was reaffirmed, even in the face of vicious predjudice.

This festival marks the essence of Jewish response to oppression, which lies in the recognition of having been irrevocably redeemed from the domination of men and ideas. While the people known as Israel have witnessed the dust blow over civilizations dating from the ancient Egyptian pharaohs to the Third Reich, the reason for its witness stays as fresh as it was in the beginning: a hunger for the truth, for the integrity of conscience. Passover has continued to transmit this spirit of inner resistance and hope through the generations.

The origins of Passover go back to the nomadic paschal sacrifice known as a *pesach*. Only much later was this word reinterpreted in Hebrew as meaning *pasach*: having passed over. In the nomadic days of Abraham, the *pesach* meal sanctified a pact. The lamb was to be eaten whole and in haste; the great concern for purity of the food (which would spoil with age) mirrored the sanctity of the communal pact. Likewise, unfermented bread (matzah) and bitter herbs (as a purgative) were elements of this concern for purity. Centuries later, these rituals were reinvested with the vision and ethics of Jewish experience. The "haste" became the haste of the Exodus, accounting for the quick-baked, unleavened matzah as well. And the symbolism of death's messenger passing over the Jewish homes that observed *Pesach* in Egypt reinterpreted the superstition about evil spirits, infusing it with monotheistic awareness.

While the symbolism of the Exodus story may seem unsophisticated to those who know it only superficially, it is a deeply imaginative rejection of the world's complex of beliefs in magic and miracle-workers. Moses is inspired to work miracles as a means of speaking to the Egyptians in the language they understand—yet everything about Moses is a fierce rejection of the typical idea of a miracle-worker. Unlike the Egyptian magician of the time, Moses' concern was first a social one: let my people go. He took no pride or pleasure in performing those acts which were part of the repertoire of Egyptian supernaturalism. The only miracles the Torah allows are archetypes of monotheism: not displays of power by supernatural gods but the use of commonplace religious modes of the time to draw attention to a new, more realistic awareness of the world. There are no gods with domains in heaven, in nature, in sea and air; it is all one wholly integrated universe.

The archetype of biblical miracles is God's revelation of concern. And the Jewish interpretation of that revelation is a constant: God does not inspire fear but the awe that leads to interpretation itself. A purely literal reading of the Bible is anathema to Judaism, with the ancient Samaritan betrayal only one instance of the enmity engendered by fundamentalism. Much of the Passover symbolism focuses upon the biblical miracles to speak to the openness of a child's imagination, and to keep open our own imaginations as well. The real miracle—present in every passage and ritual of Passover—is that we are here today. The response to this miracle is a celebration of the truths of moral conscience, which gather around the central theme of Passover: inner freedom from superstitious fear, outer freedom from the world's worship of power. Directly opposed to awesome mystery cults, the Jewish emphasis is on reality and the manifestation of conscience in everyday life. The recitation of the Hallel psalms at the Passover seder, a part of the observance for hundreds of years before the Haggadah we now use was crystallized (in the first century CE), demonstrates the range of imaginative symbolism used by Jews to express joy in freedom from idolatry.

Haggadah, which means *the aggadah* (the imaginative form of biblical interpretation, utilizing legend), is the name applied to the guide to the Passover seder, which was edited by the rabbis at Yavneh just after the Roman destruction of Jerusalem. Since the paschal sacrifice was no longer possible, the Haggadah preserved the essence of the festival by domesticating it in the same way that Jewish study and prayer became modes of transmission for the old Temple sacrifices. The seder meal itself was already an ancient tradition, and the first Haggadah was largely a distillation of traditions and texts already associated with it. The Haggadah we use today is almost identical, though expanded by later imaginative interpretations, poems, and songs.

The seder, which means the order of the service, illustrates the biblical concept of freedom and spiritual liberation. Since this liberated awareness was made possible by the physical liberation of Israel from slavery, the seder symbolically proclaims that we were commanded thousands of years ago by law to respect the freedom of all male and female servants—including the alien among the people. So joy in following the laws of the Passover seder mirrors the joy of moral self-discovery. In addition to recalling the Exodus, the desolate poverty of our condition as Hebrew slaves is remembered by a dedicated awareness of the poor and oppressed in the present.

Awareness of the universal God allowed an independence from nature, too, yet even in beholding God, Israel was free to accept or reject the Torah. It is just this independence which makes it morally imperative for each generation to rededicate itself and interpret the Exodus story in contemporary terms. The Haggadah text is the most outstanding instance of this historical process at work, as it includes examples of interpretive *aggadot* from many different times and places. The Haggadah does not record the story of the Exodus, which it quotes in part from the Torah; it is a record of the process of Jewish awareness itself. It begins with the days when we worshiped idols as "wandering Arameans" and continues through thousands of years, beyond the Roman destruction. So the Haggadah ends with the refrain "Next year in Jerusalem," which could only have been added after Jerusalem was lost.

In the portions of the Haggadah that date from Roman times, there is a messianic vision at work that the Haggadah's final refrain typifies. But the core of Jewish faith was already so solidly internalized that it was possible for Jews at that time to satirize the Roman empire. Many of the seder customs are a form of satire of Greek and Roman ways. It's not a vicious satire at all, but generous in its attribution, based as it is in Jewish self-confidence. For instance, instead of emulating the "haste" of the Exodus, we are instructed to recline on pillows when we eat, like the Roman nobility at banquets. The *afikomen* ritual is probably a satire of the Greco-Roman custom of games and entertainment with dessert—the word may derive from the ancient Greek for dessert. Our simple piece of *afikomen* is the matzah of redemption—instead of ending the meal, *afikomen* expands it with a taste of the future. Older elements of the Haggadah reflect similar transformations of pagan customs, right down to the domestic blessings themselves: invoking the "king of the universe" explodes the material sanctity invested in the "divine" kingships of worldly power.

The custom of opening the door for the prophet Elijah is an even later interpretation for the deliverance story. Elijah—like the "Age of Prophecy" itself—is to return as a messenger of redemption on Passover eve. The custom may have begun in defiance of Christian superstitions that accused the Jews of using Christian blood behind closed doors in the ghettoes on Passover ("blood libel"). The Exodus story, then, is a reminder that deliverance continues in every generation and is always a denial of the death cults, which ancient Egypt represented. Their elaborate initiation rites and mysteries of the afterlife were contradicted by the Jewish Passover, in which all the people are equally liberated. Emphasis is on life in a purposeful world and the search for understanding—not on a heavenly redemption.

Most important, the ancient custom of telling the Exodus story is directed to the children. And especially the youngest child, thereby representing the inclusion of all present, equally. It is also the imagination of the child to which the wonder of liberation speaks, and the most ancient mode of expressing poetic wonder—miraculous tales—makes these parts of the Torah as vivid to the young as to the old.

II.

The Haggadah has always been used and read in its original Hebrew. In twentieth-century America, ours may be the first time that translations are actually substituted for the originals or used as the main guide for the majority of Jews not fluent in Hebrew. These translations have traditionally been so poor in quality that their feebleness has become proverbial. Once or twice, a serious writer with an ear for English has tried his hand at an English rendition (notably Maurice Samuel in the forties), but for the most part the only art associated with the Haggadah has been the graphic illumination of it by scribes and artists.

The main reason for the bland translations is that the Haggadah is essentially a miniature anthology of works from many periods in history and in many literary styles. While the styles vary more radically than the books of the Bible—a veritable library by comparison—the Haggadah is presented as a seamless work without clear distinction as to its sources. A Jew at least somewhat familiar with Tanakh (Torah, Prophets, Writings), Talmud, Midrash, and Siddur recognizes these sources, but a translation is likely to completely lose the texture of this amazing tapestry. Not only does this create the false impression that the contents of the book were written all at the same time in some vague, ancient epoch, but the sameness of contemporary idiom creates the impression that the book was read primarily on its literal level. In fact, the Haggadah is rich with various imaginative levels, and it remains for poets to attempt translations that can approach the work in a variety of idioms, images, and forms mirroring the range of the Hebrew. Meanwhile it should be emphasized that the text has an integrity that is sadly diminished when the Haggadah is treated as if it were a sentimental antique.

In a sense, the Haggadah is a book about translation itself. Jewish translation usually took the form of interpretive commentary or paraphrase, since most Jews could read, if not understand, the original Hebrew. So the Haggadah can be seen as a collection of "interpretive translations" of the Torah through various places and centuries.

The oldest parts of the Haggadah are excerpts from the Torah (as early as nineteenth century BCE), which are included in the *midrash* (imaginative exegesis) on the Exodus story. This is an *aggadah* process itself, and the section I've translated, "To the Children," first appears in both an ancient *midrash* (third century BCE) and the Jerusalem Talmud (first century CE). The ancient core of the Haggadah is the Hallel psalms (tenth century to seventh century BCE), which were chanted after reading from the Book of Exodus. Then there are songs and poems that range from the early Middle Ages to the European Renaissance. The scholarly traditional Haggadah just completed by the Rabbinical Assembly of America (edited by Michael Strassfeld) includes a reading from Holocaust sources and from a contemporary Jew in a Soviet prison.

So today, instead of reading directly from Exodus in the Torah, or elaborating our own stories as was done in ancient Israel, we read later, midrashic interpretations to answer the Four Questions about Passover. These four questions in the mouth of the youngest child give the Haggadah its main structure and date from the same era as many of the *midrashim* (first to third centuries CE). And the answer—the story beginning with the *midrash* "We were slaves to Pharaoh in Egypt"—incorporates majestic biblical narrative into the expansive imagination of rabbinical exegesis.

Later *midrashim* give imaginative life to the earlier one I've translated by offering various interpretations of the kinds of psychological types and attitudes these children represent. "To the Children" is itself a *midrash*, interpreting four quotations from the Torah about the necessity for parents to transmit the Passover story to their children. Each of those quotations is phrased differently, so the paraphrasing of differing language characteristics by differing human characteristics is a natural step for a revitalizing commentary or translation, and *midrashim* serve as a kind of translation for their times. The Haggadah also provides a kind of domestication of the Talmud in the same way that Temple rituals are domesticated in the synagogue prayer books. Anyone who knows the Haggadah well—and it's the first book the Jewish child is exposed to—has a feel for a process at the heart of the Talmud. That process is *aggadah*, or the creative use of legend to illuminate the Torah and Talmud—to "translate" it into the active imagination of daily life. It is implicit in the nature of this creative translation process that the original Hebrew Torah and Hebrew-Aramaic Talmud can never be substituted for, but only illuminated.

Emphasis in the Haggadah is on the need for each generation to put itself in the place of the Jews in the Exodus, an ongoing liberation process. The Egypt in which Jews were slaves is not today's country of that name but modern Europe, where we were death-slaves less than forty years ago. The remnant that survived fled Europe for the most part and are in a sense redeemed in modern Israel. Not only oppression was left behind in Europe, but a whole way of life. Instead of pariah status in ghettoes, there were kibbutzim, egalitarian democracy, and new Hebrew names. The present tense of the answers to the children is as vivid as ever in the insistence of equating freedom with Jewish identity: "when I went out of Egypt/ a free man/ a Jew." In the Hebrew, the answers to the children are direct quotes from the Torah, and this quoted passage is from Exodus (13:8). While the Hebrew does not use the word "Jew," the implication is clear, especially since the equation of "slave" and "Jew" was as recent a reality in the twentieth century as it was in ancient Egypt.

"To the Children: A First-century Version" is an interpretive translation of the same part of the Haggadah but based on the Jerusalem Talmud's transmission of the *midrash*. In the more immediate context of the Talmud, which reveals the concerns of rabbis as they were faced in their own times, it appears unlikely that the interpretations of the children's attitudes apply to real children. No rabbi would think of a small child as implacably bitter (*rashah*). Their interpretations of this ancient *midrash* in first-century Jerusalem, when the Temple still stood, would probably be based on the contending ideologies within Judaism at that time. In the political idio days, the "wise" child (*chacham*) would probably refer to Greek philosophy; Hellenism had attracted many Jews. The "bitter" child (*rashah*) would be a member of the new, hostile Gnostic or "Jewish Christian" sect. The "shy" child (*tipesh*, later changed to *tam*) would be a Sadducee, who considered the oral, interpretive tradition to be old-fashioned and read the Torah on its surface level only—a "modern" fundamentalist. And the child who does not even know how to ask a question could have been the Essenes, and particularly the strict, monastic sect that withdrew to the caves at Qumran, where the Dead Sea Scrolls were found. Nevertheless, like all *midrashim*, this one is not an exact translation or an allegorical substitution in the Hellenistic fashion, but an imaginative commentary.

"A Fountain from Wilderness Stone" is one of the oldest parts of the Haggadah and was chanted at Passover long before the Haggadah was edited. It is a psalm from the group known as the Hallel (Psalms 113–18), which were originally chanted by the Levites in the Temple. The chanting of the Hallel at the home Passover meal was probably the first instance of the domestic use of Temple liturgy. Later, during the Second Jewish Commonwealth, the Hallel was recited in the synagogue on all festivals, as it is today. But, in those days, the Passover story was not yet focused on the Exodus; the paschal sacrifice was still offered in the Temple, and its covenant symbolism was preeminent. So the 114th Psalm, which is the one most identified with Passover now because it refers to the Exodus, was not prominent in the ancient Pesach pilgrimage festival. In fact, the derivation of the term "Passover" from "Pesach" was made during later Talmudic days precisely to place the festival emphasis on the Exodus and diminish the relevance of the paschal sacrifice, which was rendered obsolete after the Temple's destruction.

The character of the Hallel psalms, poems of thanskgiving, allows for the expansive imagery in Psalm 114. The anthropomorphic hills are typically ancient imagery, but the psalmist's usage transforms them into an exuberant affirmation of monotheistic awareness: like the desert miracles themselves, they are clearly poeticized. The events related—crossing the Sea of Reeds, and the later parallels of crossing the Jordan into Israel and then the Kingdom of Israel (or Judah) itself—refer to the communal history in a heady, more personalized way than does the Torah. To clarify the poet's animation of historical events, I've sharpened the focus of personal surprise and exultation, which is reflected in the paralleling of fanciful Israelite scenery with the deeply felt reality of the desert miracles, which end the poem. I've done this by drawing out the original implication of simple awe in having *arrived*, in being at home in the land. This seems an appropriate interpretation for Passover in these days of a renewed Israel.

Passover had become one of the two major seasonal festivals (along with Sukkot) of the Second Jewish Commonwealth. They were major pilgrimage festivals; and Jews would come long distances to stay in Jerusalem and visit the Temple. While Sukkot was diminished by the loss of Temple and independence, Passover became the major festival of the Diaspora. Connected more with the deliverance of the people than national independence, the emphasis in Passover shifted to hope for the future. Though the harvest seasons were different in the lands of exile, the agricultural aspect of Passover was natural to recall, since it coincided with spring. The early rabbis strengthened the association with spring and rebirth by making the Song of Songs the scroll for Passover. It is read in the synagogue on the festival Shabbat, and excerpts from it are often included in the Haggadah for reading at the seder. In addition, the messianic vision implied by the allegorical interpretation of the Song of Songs served Passover well. This allegorical reading was ingrained in the work by the time of the first Aramaic targum (translation, paraphrase), and so we can assume this was the only way Jews knew it after the return from Babylon in the sixth century BCE. All the targums to the Song of Songs are free allegorical translations, some taking greater liberties with the Hebrew text than the oldest midrashic Hebrew commentaries.

In tune with Passover's historical and agricultural dimensions, "All My Memories Melt into You" reflects both aspects of the flowering of Israel: indigenous Canaanite imagery testifying to Israel's secure root in the land and the springtime reawakening of a passion for life. Much of the imagery of the Song of Songs comes from ancient Canaanite ritual songs concerning the annual marriage rites of the pagan fertility gods. Hebrew poets took this indigenous imagery and transformed it into an immediate, sensual awareness of the divine passion in Judaism. The emotional feeling (rather than pious theology) for the Torah was easily allegorized.

To read these biblical songs or poems as secular love songs, as some scholars have suggested they originally were, is also to allegorize them, though in a modern mode. Since the pagan lovers in the original imagery were gods, not mortals, their ritualized passion was not divisible into the idiomatic sense of dynamic relationships between two human beings. Though the poems may have later been used in Canaanite wedding rites on the folk level, their imagery reflects the common type of poeticized exaggeration that was a domestication of the pagan liturgical style: the classic high literature of the times.

In "All My Memories Melt into You" I've tried to capture a sense of both the modern, literal interpretation, and the traditional, allegorical one in which God is speaking to his love, the people Israel. The Jewish sense of allegory is different not only from Hellenistic allegory but from the Western idea of allegory coming from medieval Europe. The imagery in the Song of Songs remains palpably real: the love for the physical reality of the Torah scroll, its columns, even its wooden handles, is as passionately felt—and as stylized in imagery—as the legs of a lover. And the historical love affair between God and the people Israel unfolds dramatically in the idiom of emotional anxiety.

The oneness of Israel's God, the presence behind time and space, creation and history, is at the core of "All My Memories Melt into You," reflecting the historical and religious concerns of Passover. This chapter of Song of Songs ends, like the Haggadah and the seder service itself, with Israel's timeless affirmation of faith in human redemption from idolatry, oppression, and disbelief.

TO THE CHILDREN

(The Haggadah and The Talmud)

We are reminded to teach our children
by the Torah
in four different verses and ways
like four different children

one child is wise
one child is bitter, one child is shy
and one child does not know enough
to ask a question

the wise one—what does he ask?
what is the meaning of these rules
these special laws and customs you are commanded
to follow by the Lord our God?

(this one seems to know that God
the creator
and the God of Israel
are one)

and now you must tell this child
each and every law of Pesach
the customs and traditions
right down to the end

nothing remains to be eaten
after the *afikomen* matzah
that is our dessert
rich with the lingering memory

of the paschal lamb
that was eaten in the days of freedom
in Israel, where we desired
to taste the sweetness of God's word

the bitter one—what does he ask?
why do you follow this dull old ritual?
you, not *him*, for he is alienated
withdrawn from the sense of community

and like a little god of his own
he brings himself out of Israel
into an empty desert, a slavish illusion
of having been independently created

yet since he only survives
by attacking his own roots
you should confront him also
wake him up, say

because of what God did for me
when I was brought out of slavery in Egypt—
for *me*, not *him*—had he been there
he would not have been redeemed

he would choose the reality of slavehood
to remain locked in the memoryless present
blind in the steam of his own bitterness
generating its illusions of independence

the shy one—what does he ask?
what's this?
and to him you will say
the Lord stretched out his hand

to bring us out of Egypt
out of the world's greatest power
where we were deep in slavery—
and we are here by the strength of his presence

now to the one who does not know enough
to ask a question—you will answer him
simply by beginning to read
just what the Torah says:

and you will tell your child
on that day—when you are gathered
together in the presence of tradition—
this is happening now

because of what God did for me
when I went out of Egypt
a free man
a Jew.

TO THE CHILDREN: A First-century Version

We are reminded to speak out
by the Torah
in four different verses and ways
to four different fellow Jews

one man is shrewd
one man is our hater
one is a fool
one refuses to even speak to us

the shrewd one—what does he say?
what is the philosophical basis
for these rules, laws and customs you feel
God himself commanded us?

and you must tell this man
each and every law of Pesach
the customs and traditions
exact and in detail, from first to last . . .

the hater—what does he say?
why do you need such outdated rituals?
you, not *him*, for he has superior wisdom
and hates his father and mother

you should set this one's teeth on edge
remind him of how he twists his heritage
in order to be his own slave-master
and dominate us, with his false comforting . . .

the fool—what does he say?
does this still mean something?
no serious discussion beyond surface truths
will penetrate his wooden brain

he believes he hears only the fundamental
but his ears are open
to merely the sound of what he hears—
you must awaken his sense of awe . . .

now to the one who refuses
to speak to us—supply him
with the information he needs:
lay the book before him. . . .

A FOUNTAIN FROM WILDERNESS STONE
(The Book of Psalms and The Haggadah)

When Israel came out of Egypt
like a child suddenly free
from a people of strange speech

Judah became a home
for the Children of Israel
as they became a Sanctuary

for the God of their fathers—
the House of Israel
were brought into the open

and as the Sea saw them coming
it ran from the sight
the Jordan stopped dead in its tracks

mountains leaped like frightened rams
hills were a scattering flock
of lambs

What was so alarming, Sea?
Jordan, what vision
drained your strength away?

Mountains, why did you quake
like fearful rams?
Hills, why did you jump like lambs?

All earth, tremble
in the presence
of your maker

it was the God of Jacob
and he is here
all around you

a sudden pool of water
from a desert rock
a fountain from wilderness stone—

life from a heart of stone
and from bitter tears
a sweet land.

(Psalm 114)

ALL MY MEMORIES MELT INTO YOU
(The Song of Songs)

I will be in my garden
as I am deep within you
my bride

as if you are my sister
I am rich in spices—
as if my bride, I pluck fresh myrrh

I am rich with honey
and I will eat the honeycomb whole
as well

I will have my wine, my bride
and it is pure, my sister
as milk and honey

friend, you will eat
you will drink deeply, lover
you will be rich with love, my dearest friend

I was asleep
but the soul within me
stayed awake

like my heart—true to a timeless rhythm
to which I still respond—
listen, a gentle knocking

like my heart's beating—
Open to me, my love
my purest image, sister, dove

all I can imagine—my head is drenched
with dew, all my memories
melt into you

I would walk through nights of blinding rain
all doors locked to my presence
I would be happy in blackest exile

knowing you alone would not reject me
never forget
not turn away—

*

But I've undone the robe of devotion
where I wrapped my naked heart before you—
how can I rise to your presence?

I've washed the feet that were tired and dirty
when I walked in the reality of your presence—
how can I stand and face myself?

*

My love who came inside me
whom I held firmly
whose hand was on the lock of my being

removed his arms
pulled his hand away—
I awoke and

I was drawn to him
a softness spread in me
I was open within

and then I was desolate and empty
he had gone
my heart leapt from my breast

I ran to the door
my soul overwhelmed me
my hands were drenched, as if with perfume
it was my love for him—
the lock was wet with the myrrh
of my devotion

I opened for my love
I alone was open to him
but he had gone

the one for whom I trembled
heard it from my lips
how I had turned from him when

I thought I was alone—
suddenly my soul no longer knew me
just as I had forgotten him

I was riveted with anxiety
I was as lifeless as an empty robe
I couldn't move

my feet were a statue's feet
I was lifeless clay
I was naked earth

then I wandered through the streets
looking for signs of his nearness
seeing nothing

I called, I cried
desperate for his closeness
hearing only silence

only my enemies heard me, like watchmen
patrolling my city's walls
who found me in night gown

who saw me vulnerable and alone
who struck me down
I was wounded for my distraction

my robe my dignity stripped away
I could not even pray
my heart was in my mouth

but now, nations of the world, I warn you
when you see my love
when you turn toward Jerusalem

you will say I bore all for him
the pain and loss was love for him
I was his to the core

"But what makes your love any better than ours
what makes you so beautiful
that he leaves you, and you search for him?

How is your love better than any other
that you stoop from your ivory tower
daring to warn us?"

My love is white with radiance
red with vigorous strength
unmistakable—a banner leading the way

over the heads of a great army
and his head more inspiring than a crown of gold
his hair a raven-black flame

a dove's eyes, clear
beside a soothing river
reflecting its depth, brimming

pools of tenderness—
indestructible jewels
set in whites of kindness

his gaze a penetrating shaft of light
so deft
it is milk—warm and familiar

his words are riverbanks, firm
lush spice beds
a lingering perfume

to remind you of his lips
which are roses
his beard a soft bed of grass

to lean against like a page of his words
bathed in transparent dew
flowing with myrrh

his arms form a vessel of gold
to hold me secure
as a voyager to Tarshish

his will is a sail
and his desires
are a steady wind

his belly is polished ivory—
and strong, clear as azure
is his skin—a cloudless sky

his legs are firm columns
fine as marble
and his feet like golden pedestals—

columns of a scroll, words of spun gold—
his appearance naturally noble as
Lebanon cedars swaying in the breeze

his breath a delicious breeze
words a golden nectar
sustenance and delight

he is altogether delightful—
this is my love
and this my true friend

who never abandons me
a love so pure
you will know it unmistakably

when you turn toward Jerusalem
nations of the world
and all your sons and daughters.

(Chapter 5)

JEREMIAH

HOLOCAUST DAY

TO PUT YOUR MOUTH TO DUST
(The Book of Lamentations)

The very word "holocaust" challenges the existence of anything significantly human: a truth, justice, or morality that lifts humanity above self-interest. The descent into murder by the civilizations of Europe under the Germans was actually the complete negation of the biblical word meaning holocaust. The ancient Jewish concept of a holocaust is of a sacred gift, given in reverence of God. The modern Holocaust sacrifice of Jewish people was not a burnt offering, a communion with God, but a denial of humanity and a judgment of God's absence.

So, it is the Jews who acknowledge God's presence by reaffirming humanity via their tradition. The possible absence of God, his hiddenness, is part of the Jewish understanding of the world—rooted in experience, true to a historical, reality, and based on a vision of moral justice. Hence, the term Holocaust, in its adoption by Jews for the European mass murder, is both a protest and a life-affirming avowal which can best be made in a Jewish context.

Precedent for the Jewish tradition of speaking out was well established by the time of an ancient catastrophe: the destruction of Israel and Judah by Assyria and Babylon, culminating in the Temple's destruction, the Jerusalem massacres, and the mass exile of 586 BCE. The witness that has come down to us, Eichah, or the Book of Lamentations, was composed not long afterward. It was based on earlier forms of lament, but fused an expression of deep despair with deep care for God. Just as the term Holocaust contains a sense of both protest and affirmation, the two extremes of reverence and despair are always within the realm of Jewish response. Lamentations became the liturgy of the sacred day internalizing the First Temple's destruction: Tisha b'Av (the ninth of Av).

The memorial day of Tisha b'Av grew in stature through the later survivals of catastrophe in Jewish history. Today it remains the second major fast day, after Yom Kippur, and Lamentations is chanted in all synagogues around the world on that day. In Israel, the day is marked by gatherings at the Western Wall, in Jerusalem, a remnant of the Second Temple.

In the aftermath of genocidal holocaust, in 1951 (expanded in 1961), the state of Israel designated the first modern religious observance on the Jewish calendar as Yom ha-Shoah: Holocaust Day. The ancient Hebrew term *shoah* was transformed, given a new resonance, one whose deep echoes are contained within Jewish tradition. Like all events in Jewish history, it can be anchored—like the word itself—in the Torah. But no distinctive liturgy or form of observance has yet been confirmed, beyond the powerful observance of silence throughout Israel, as sirens blast for two minutes at noon and the entire nation comes to a halt. In America, the holiday has so far been acknowledged in Shabbat sermons and by the showing of Holocaust documentaries. Recently, a Presidential Commission on Holocaust Memorials has honored the day with observances in the Capital, designating it "International Holocaust Day."

The major effort to absorb Yom ha-Shoah within the tradition during the last decade was focused on an Israeli proposal to incorporate it with Tisha b'Av, investing the latter with renewed significance. The Israeli Prime Minister is one of the advocates of observing Yom ha-Shoah on Tisha b'Av. While the proposal is still a source of controversy, the idea itself infuses Lamentations with new meaning. I've set out to take the proposal further, to reinvest Lamentations with modern relevance, so it can be used as a text for Yom ha-Shoah.

As with Yom Kippur, the fasting on Tisha b'Av is not the day's primary observance. Tisha b'Av is basically a day of mourning for the destruction of Jerusalem, and the chanting of the Book of Lamentations is the central part of its service. During the medieval centuries of European degradation, at its worst during the Crusades and the Inquisition, new compositions by Jewish poets, modeled on the biblical laments and called *kinot*, were appended to the reading of Lamentations. In Sephardic ritual throughout the world, the Book of Job is also chanted on Tisha b'Av. Although he suffers terribly, and refuses to be silenced with easy answers, Job's belief in moral justice and God's presence is never in doubt. His speaking out comes from the anguish of not knowing the charge against him, from being at a loss as to why this catastrophe is happening to him. Yet Job never turns from directly facing the reality of his experience; he does not want to repress it, escape it, or simplify it. On Tisha b'Av, Job is like the people Israel. His torture is beyond imagination, but the integrity of his conscience is unshakable.

Through the Book of Lamentations, we witness the depth of Jewish conscience as it beholds a God who allows his own Temple to be destroyed. Within a generation of this event, while still a living memory, Jewish poets were able to compose these inspired biblical laments, speaking out against the worldly injustice from a faith rooted in the sense of a divine moral justice. For this was not *a* god, not a tribal or imperial god, but *the* God, the one creator the whole world is responsible to. This was the monotheistic conscience in a darkened world, 2,500 years ago, darkened again in our time by the hands of self-deified men.

The human extremes of despair and joyous awe are both spoken for in Lamentations. The event of holocaust is never completely justified; there is no easy comfort in absolute answers. But the response is deeply felt on personal terms: it is we who are the losers, and God also feels the loss, and we share the disaster and pain. With open eyes we blame ourselves, not in simplistic concepts of sin, or pagan concepts of retribution, or in the atheistic sense of being "victims of fate" (as the ancient Greeks were victims of the gods' rivalry). We take on the sense of blame in order to feel the depth of loss for the whole world—to remain open to the reality of an imperfect and difficult world.

These laments were not composed out of thin air. The form of a lament existed at the roots of early civilization. Sumerian laments over the destruction of cities were being composed while Abraham was leaving for Canaan, and sometimes these compositions were put into the mouth of the ruined city's pagan goddess. The Jewish poets took this universal form and transformed it into a vehicle of great poetry, based on a monotheistic vision of an interdependent mankind. It is the daughter of Zion who laments in parts of the book, and she is no goddess but only a beautiful metaphor conveying the feelings of loss—the loss of real people, as well as homeland.

Nothing—no gods, no men—comes between God and man in Jewish expression. Men and women are bound to speak out as witnesses, directly to God. Even the unspeakable is given voice by ordinary, living people, to counteract the mysteries, silences, and abandonments of the world's sacred gods and idols. Silence, even before a generation had passed, was almost unthinkable for a people who recorded and elaborated God's word. There were no idols or events too sacred for Jewish response. To the Jewish poet, language was as much a vehicle for communion among people as it was between man and God.

The ancient form of a lament in Hebrew was made flexible enough to carry a sense of human protest and outrage, as well as awe and admiration—beyond solace, beyond mourning, it is bearing witness. And with a monotheistic consciousness, a sense of the whole world before one creator, the people Israel itself became a witness to the world. Unlike the modern, secular context, with its frail belief in "mankind" as well as a pale humanitarianism easily dumbfounded before the spectacle of a debased civilization, the Jewish context called for unflinching witness. And a renewal of witness takes the form of observance, a speaking out from the depth of the Jewish poetic tradition.

Each of the five chapters of the Book of Lamentations is a separate lament. I've focused on the third chapter because it is the most personal. My English version can be read privately or, perhaps, as a public, responsive reading. I wanted to parallel the ancient liturgical form by using a form of stanza and grouping that would make it easy to read aloud. And I've concentrated on the phrasing of modern speech, making the biblical text sound as speakable as the chanting in Hebrew.

Lamentations is also read in the Catholic Church, from the Latin translation, as the liturgy for Ash Wednesday. In this contemporary English renewal, Lamentations may help reanchor a Jewish observance—while the Hebrew original retains the dominant usage, on Tisha b'Av. Just as the Book of Lamentations led to later laments (*kinot*) being freely based upon it, modern literary responses also may expand from—and in—a great tradition.

The original Hebrew is built upon a special rhythmic and acrostic form. I've based this translation's phrasing on the Hebrew meter, and its sections on the acrostic form. Each section of five stanzas is designated with a letter of the Hebrew alphabet (*aleph, bet,* etc.); the sequence runs through the entire alphabet as inexorably as the full range of human emotions, from despair to praise, is played out.

Additional liturgy suitable for Yom ha-Shoah may be anchored in the biblical works read during the Shabbats of remembrance before Tisha b'Av as well as other Yizkors (remembrances), such as before Purim. Psalms, the prophets Ezekiel, Jeremiah, and Isaiah (particularly the "suffering servant" chapters), Daniel, Esther, and the Kaddish are other appropriate texts. The Kaddish has become a paradigm of response to personal tragedy in Jewish observance: the triumphant affirmation of life in the face of death, transforming loss into awe and reverence.

The extremes of desolation and joy are both active in the Jewish collective conscience, unembraceable extremes which are acknowledged by the spirit of renewal. Jewish observance of the ancient festivals represents a commitment to historical reality, and our present reality requires a refusal to turn away from the traumatic degradation of twentieth-century history. Jewish observance does not allow escape into the recent triumphs of American affluence or Israel's rebirth. Israel's Independence Day celebration was balanced by the creation of Yom ha-Shoah, and Israel's renewal remains a witness to the Holocaust. The form of observance for this day must also be discovered in the process of renewal, and in the restorative power of literary parallels.

TO PUT YOUR MOUTH TO DUST
(The Book of Lamentations)

Aleph

It is I who have seen
with just a man's eyes

suffering beyond the power of men
to know is there

a wrath so deep
we are struck dumb

and we are sheep
seized by animal terror

defenseless before a world unleashed
from anything human

we have seen its frenzy raised like an arm
but we feel our shepherd's blow

Bet

He has led me into darkness
a valley no light can reach

nothing to illumine the smallest step I take
though I follow what he alone may teach

he has turned against me
with the arm that pointed my way

it is I alone who felt his hand
all sleepless night and day again

he reduced me to skin and bones
my skin was paper for his heavy hand

I was under siege
I was herded into ghettoes

Ghimel

My mind was utterly stranded
surrounded by seas of poverty

he let me sit in the dark
until I could not think

I was sealed up in a tomb
with the ancient dead

I was fenced in like sheep
I was locked in an empty room

I was bound in chains
I could not turn around

I could not stand up to pray
he had turned away

Dalet

I would cry after him for help
my throat was dry as clay

all my hopes came to roadblocks
all my dreams to barbed wire

inside myself I was exposed in a desert
all my ways arrived at despair

he was a scorpion in my path
a lion crouching in the brush

he had become my nightmare
a mad bear in my tracks

a cancer waiting inside me
a fear of being torn to pieces

Hey

He had mauled my confidence
I was a living horror

all the world turned its eyes away
I crawled in the desert

I was his target
I was pinned in the center of his sight

I was pierced in my vital organs
I had lost control of my bowels

I was a laughingstock to the world
he made me their cruelest joke

he passed me the cup of bitterness
he made me drunk with tears

Vav

I was dazed with wormwood
I was in a deadly stupor

he pressed my face in the dust
I had ground my teeth to bits

I have woken with my heart in pieces
I have breakfasted on ashes

my life was pulled from my grasp
my soul was in exile

I was a hollow shell
I was a stranger to myself

peace was a dry husk, an empty word
I was blown in the wind

Zayen

I forgot what goodness means
shalom meant nothing to me

and I thought: my spirit is dead
hope in God is beyond me

I was broken down, mumbling
I was shattered by anxiety

the more I thought about my suffering—
remembering the agony of my losses—

the more I tasted wormwood
turning to poison within me

and now, still, I remember everything
my soul staggers into exile:

Het

Memory the weight on my back
and deep in my breast every crushing detail

I cannot close my eyes before it
I cannot rise from my bed

and yet I do each day
and I rouse my heart

that the memory itself so vividly lives
awakens a deathless hope

loving-kindness like air
cannot be used up

though I breathe heavily, locked in a room
beyond the wall a wind blows freely

Tet

The Lord's mercy brings a new morning
each day awakens the thought of him

though I'm buried in nights of doubt
day returns faithfully—he's always there

"The Lord is all that I have"
calls my soul and my heart responds

my hope lives within, infinite as mercy
how else could I *remember* it!

the Lord is good to me
because I do not turn and run

his goodness does not disappear
to the heart turning to him:

Yod

Remembering in the turning
trusting in the memory

how good to find patience
to let rejected hope return

and how good to learn
to bear the burden young

to sit silent and alone
when the weight falls on your shoulders

to feel the weight of your maker
as all hope seems lost

to put your mouth to dust
(perhaps living is still worthwhile)

*

To turn you cheek to its striker
to be overwhelmed by abuse

to face the worst
to drink your fill of disgrace

to swallow mockery of things held dear
to survive the poison of humiliation

*

Kaph

How good to be desolate and alone
because the Lord does not reject forever

after the intensity of anger
mercy returns in a firm embrace

because his love lasts forever
beyond anything we can know

no matter how far away
he does not abandon his creation

we were not tormented lightly
yet nothing in him desired suffering

he didn't desire to make us earth's prisoners
returning to the dust at our feet

Lamed

And when men lower us in their eyes
cheapen our right to be ourselves

when we are brutalized by "universal" justice
subverting the word "justice" itself

because men believe they are not seen
are not in God's presence when they judge

(even with their hands laid upon bibles
their interest devout self-interest)

and when we are tormented for being different
by laws of idol or human supremacy

his justice is brutally mocked
he has not desired it:

Mem

His own creation abandoning him
is a horror

but men can say and do as they want
they can act like gods: speak and it comes to pass

but they become heartless idols speaking
they will pass into dust and silence

they couldn't have opened their eyes
if the Lord did not desire it

and they strut in iron over us
yet the Lord does not will it—

because the words for good and evil
both came from him

Nun

We the living have a complaint
ignorance

a strong man or woman remembers
their weakness

instead of running from the past
turn to face the source

open your heart on the rough path of knowing
open your mind on the hard road understanding

the solid ground supports
firm trust

let us search our ways
examine the difficulties within:

Samech

Where the will and faith turn bitter
repent that loss, return to him

take your heart in your hands
lift it high

sweetness flows from a broken heart
to heaven

we have hurt and destroyed
in self-righteous ignorance

Lord, we were lost in clouds of our own making
you could not forgive this

you knocked us down
you exposed us to your anger:

Pey

You were hidden behind it
we were slaughtered without mercy

the earth was a vast pen for us
you were hidden beyond the clouds

our prayers were hollow echoes
our hopes were crushed flowers

littering the ground like discolored pages
ripped from prayer books

you had made us garbage
in the world's eyes

human refuse
reeking in a senseless world

Ayen

Our misery only enraged them
all our enemies gathered to jeer us

we were beaten as a whining dog
our blood pounded in our ears

their mouths were opened wide
pouring our hatred

the world in open chorus
blind and shameless

we had fallen into a hole
the world was a hunter's pit

death was our horizon
terror as far as our eyes could see

Tzaddik

A dam burst in my eyes
to see the heart of my people broken

the daughter of my people terrorized
her defenses breached, pride swept away

all the built-up pressure released
like a river that runs forever

until the Lord looks down
to me

what I see with my own eyes
floods my mind, sickens me

I am swept up in the wake
of my daughter's despair

Qoph

I was brought down for no reason
like a bird with a stone

by people who hate me just for being
again they bring me down, again

I am thrown into a pit
a stone is rolled over me

I who sing to the sky
am not to breathe

the nations of the world were like water
flowing over my head

to whom could I turn
I said to myself "I am gone"

Resh

In the deepest pit, Lord
I was drowning, alone

in the depths of abandonment
yet your name was on my lips

and you knew I was there
do not turn your ear from my groaning

whenever I turned to prayer
I felt you suddenly near

as if you said "do not fear"
Lord, you restored my soul

you were there and I knew
I could never be disowned

Shin

You gave me the right to be myself
and you've seen men take it away

you've seen the hands across my mouth
Lord, speak for me and clear my name

even words have been subverted
I was brought to the bar of injustice

you saw their barbarous vengeance
you saw their final solution

my life was a living death
I was butchered for you

my death was the solution to all their problems
all their imagination was brought to my dying

Tauf

You heard their hatred crafted against me
as shameless as daily prayers

holy alliances condemning me
you saw the papers drawn up openly

their minds and their mouths fastened on me
like bloodsuckers

behind my back or in their company
I was spittle on their lips

in conference or on the street
I am the scapegoat uniting them

I lighten their labors
I am the guinea pig of their salvation

*

For the hands they raise to slaughter us
with your hand, Lord, strike them deeply within

let their pride be the poison they swallow
their hearts are stones, their minds tombstones

etched there forever let all their words mock them
with their bloody thoughts spilling into silent dust.

*

(Chapter 3)

RUTH

SHAVUOT

THE BOOK OF RUTH

I.

Of the major biblical festivals, Shavuot was the last to take on deeper historical significance. Through Second Temple times, it remained primarily a seasonal festival with the emphasis on its agricultural aspect. It celebrated the end of the grain harvest—*shavuot* means weeks, the period of time culminating in the harvest and offering of firstfruits. The Temple ritual for this offering symbolized the uniquely Jewish covenant relationship with God, a pact of mutual dependence and respect. This covenant was not between servants and an overlord or divine king: it represented an understanding freely chosen and an eternally binding pact mutually embraced. While this was a powerfully new conception in the world, it was so embedded in ancient Jewish culture that its spiritual relevance to Shavuot did not become elaborated until after the Roman destruction and consequent dispersion from Temple and land.

With the loss of land, the spiritual side of the festival was interpreted as reaching back to the revelation at Sinai. Weeks of grain harvest now corresponded to weeks in the desert from the time of freedom out of Egypt to the receiving of the Torah (in the seed of the Ten Commandments) at Sinai. The event at Mount Sinai, where the people of Israel heard the word of the Lord, was the foundation for the community of Israel. So Shavuot was also known more recently in parts of the Diaspora as Pentecost—the Jewish version of the Christian foundation for its Church.

The spiritual harvest that is Shavuot—the acceptance of the Torah and covenant—was cultivated at a time in history when the depth of Israel's memory was crucial. This era, near the Roman dispersion, was a ripe one for poetic memory and interpretation. Just as the original, agricultural festival of Shavuot could only have been celebrated after the settling of Israel, so the later interpretation could only have been made after the Torah had become firmly rooted in the people of Israel—a democratizing process carried out by the Pharisees and brought to fruition by the early rabbis of the Diaspora.

Today, Shavuot resonates with both the culture and the memory of ancient Israel. The custom of decorating the synagogue with green branches and flowers reflects the agricultural origin, and the custom of *Tikkun* echoes the strength of mystical spirit during centuries of Diaspora days. *Tikkun* means the work of repairing and refers to the custom of staying up all night to read—beginning at midnight—a book containing the first and last verses of all the biblical books, Talmudic tractates, and additional mystical compositions from the Zohar, as well as prayers and poems connected to the 613 *mitzvot* (commandments, or good deeds) of the Halachah (Oral Torah, rooted in God's revelation at Sinai and growing from the Ten Commandments). On the second night of Shavuot, the Tikkun is mirrored by an evening reading of the entire Book of Psalms, remembering the death of David, with its messianic promise of eventual redemption from his seed. The importance to Shavuot of King David and messianic hope was also underlined when the Book of Ruth was chosen as the festival scroll.

The seven weeks between the second night of Passover (the traditional date for the beginning of the harvest and the ancient offering of the first sheaf) and Shavuot (the end of the harvest and the ancient offering of newly baked bread) are a period of counting of days. There is a spiritual edge to these days, because they correspond to the period of anticipation between the redemption from Egypt and the revelation at Sinai—an equal number of days, according to interpretations of the Torah's Book of Exodus. Because of the prominent mystical side to Shavuot, many additional symbolic interpretations encompass it.

II.

Both the harvest and the convenant themes of Shavuot are reflected in the Book of Ruth, which is read in the synagogue. The story of Ruth is older than that of Esther or Judith, and its final author had a keener ear for the poetics of biblical narrative. Of the essence in this narrative is a sensitive economy of words. Instead of the verbal extravagance of Esther, or the dramatic flair of Judith, we have an intensity of scene and image, woven around key themes. The marriage of the Book of Ruth and the festival of Shavuot keeps these themes fresh in our minds, as the delicate development of plot unfolds in the group chanting in the synagogue. The book is a literary masterpiece, absorbing elements of poetic parallelism and evolving a rhythm of key images and word patterns. Its brief length has the expansive quality of a book, in its historical and prophetic resonance.

In the first chapter, Ruth forgoes the prospect of "a home of kindness/ in the house of a loving husband" for an act of *chesed* (loving-kindness). Ruth chooses to stay in the house of her mother-in-law, honoring her dead husband's memory—she has acquired from them a love (demonstrated in the character of Naomi) that is stronger than her ties to her homeland. She embraces the heart of Judaism—not primarily its rituals and culture but the principle of *chesed* stemming from covenant ethics, at the core of biblical faith. Far from encouraging her daughter-in-law to even think of accepting the Jewish people, Naomi warns her of hardship and advises her to turn back. But Ruth accepts Judaism and participates in the covenant by performing an act of *chesed*.

Since the essence of *chesed* is a dynamic, continuous frame of awareness, Ruth performs more than one act of loving-kindness. The first is to honor the family of her mother-in-law, left without an heir to perpetuate it. By returning to Bethlehem with Naomi, Ruth distinguishes her mother-in-law and Jewish tradition by following the kinship customs that may redeem the family name. The name, or house, is tied to the land, in the form of property rights owned by her deceased father-in-law. So both the land and the promise of descendants must be renewed, and Ruth prepares the way for both by the devotion she shows Naomi. This devotion becomes literally visualized as Ruth goes out to glean in the fields. To the women of Bethlehem, Ruth becomes known as a "woman of valor," and an older, more literal model than Judith during the Maccabean age.

Another act of *chesed* is the offer of marriage to Boaz, a legal kin (perhaps a cousin to her deceased husband). Boaz does not have to accept her (this is not a case of levirate marriage law), and so Ruth places herself in a vulnerable position by initiating the proposal.

The vulnerability of Ruth's position with Boaz provides the emotional drama to the book. We are already aware of Boaz's kindness to her in the fields, but the motivation for it remains implicit, perhaps even tinted with tender shades of love's affection. The drama then becomes explicit at the threshing floor—the dramatic tension is between the visual description of the personal encounter and the underlying strength of conscience both characters display. The encounter is full of tender, vulnerable feelings, but the risks are much higher than personal fulfillment. Perpetuation of a nation is metaphorically in the balance (though in a subtle way that does not upset the non-moralizing, delicate balance of the story), and the love that Boaz and Ruth demonstrate is not first to each other but to individual conscience—the seedbed of a Jewish heritage.

The symbolic act of uncovering Boaz's legs (or feet, though the latter word does not convey the proper note of apprehension) so that he wakes of his own accord is paralleled later in the ritual act of rejection by the closest kin-redeemer, as he passes on his right to redeem Naomi's land. He takes off his sandal to symbolize his renunciation, rejecting the position of vulnerability. In all cases, though, the right of individual choice and commitment is subtly underscored, paralleling the equality of roles in a covenant agreement. And here we have an ethical paradigm for all Jewish covenant relationships, flowing from the one between God and the people Israel, rooted in individual conscience.

Boaz takes over the role of kin-redeemer, performing an act of *chesed* to match Ruth's, for he is not obliged to marry her. Of course we sense they are truly in love, but their mutual acceptance of the Jewish tradition of loving-kindness also allows Boaz to say: "this name will not disappear." That name comes to represent a link in the chain of Israel that gives birth to the fulfillment of God's promise in the covenant, a right to live in the land of Israel. This union with the land is here deeply poeticized and in a spirit captured by the Shavuot festival: King David, the embodiment of Jewish struggle for independence, will be born as descendant of Ruth and Boaz. So the real harvest will also yield a spiritual harvest—but, instead of formal ritual, we feel the immediacy of this spirit in the love and joy of parents for the birth of their child.

This child from Bethlehem who will become the grandfather of David is a harvest of love, not only for his parents but for Jewish tradition as well, symbolized by Naomi, the grandmother, as she takes Ruth's child to her breast: "a son is born to Naomi." In the words of the women of the city, "the Lord be blessed/ whose kindness has not ceased/ to this day, never leaving you/ bereft of a redeemer." The word "redeem" here, and throughout the story, is manifested in the physical necessity of daily life. Redeeming is an aspect of contractual ethics between people, both in dealings of property and in family relations. And it is a vital aspect of the tradition of loving-kindness, of *chesed*. The emphasis falls equally on the physical and the spiritual—it was "Rachel and Leah/ who built the house in Israel," women who chose to serve Israel in a palpable way.

Just as an act of redemption leads to the birth of a child and a renewed claim to the land, in a spiritual sense the people of Israel are promised a redeemer to fulfill their covenant with God. King David is the model of this redeemer in Jewish tradition. And it is not a "theological" David who dramatizes the genealogy at the end of the Book of Ruth, but a beloved, human child. Just as a contractual covenant among people depends on mutual respect, the covenant between God and Israel at Sinai is rooted in a bond of *chesed*. This loving-kindness is a seed that grows into the ethical core of Judaism and a promise of a messianic age in earthly terms of reality—not a heavenly redemption, but an era of goodwill among all people living on earth.

It was natural for the festival of Shavuot, celebrating the revelation of the Ten Commandments at Sinai (themselves like the firstfruits of the covenant), to take on the mystical attributes of redemption as well. In a metaphor the Talmud creates, King David died on Shavuot and one of his descendants yet to come will be born on that day. That descendant will be here when the love of conscience displayed by Boaz and Ruth governs the lives of all men and women.

A covenant must be accepted freely by both parties, and, in the same way, Ruth accepts Judaism while she is accepted into the people Israel. Ruth's non-Jewish background is mitigated by her demonstration of a loving conscience. In the same way, again Israel is a witness to God's revelation for mankind as a whole.

The ethical practice of *chesed* is also metaphorically present in the Book of Ruth in the role of the witnesses at the "trial" and betrothal of Boaz and Ruth—"today, in this assembly/ you are witnesses." There is nothing mystical or symbolic in this role of witness. It is a palpable feeling for justice that pervades the book. These witnesses in Ruth's day parallel both the earlier witnesses at Sinai and the continuing process as it reaches into our own day. So it is a process of continuing witness that is commemorated at the festival of Shavuot: the tradition says every Jew stood at Sinai.

Chapter 1

And it was back in the Days of Judges
when the law was not always lived
as the judges received it
and it was a time of famine
ravaging the land

There was a man, then
of Bethlehem, in Judah, who left
wandering to foreign soil, in Moab
with his wife and two sons—
this man was named Elimelech
and his wife, Naomi
and two sons, Mahlon and Kilyon
and they were Ephraimites, established Bethlehem Jews

They reached the fertile land in Moab
sojourning, then settling there
Elimelech, the man who had been husband
to Naomi, died, and she was left there
but stayed on, with her two sons

The sons settled down in Moab
each marrying a Moabite woman
one was named Orpah
and the second, Ruth
and for ten years they lived on there

But the two sons, Mahlon and Kilyon
also died, and Naomi was left there
without husband, without children

The woman, with her daughters-in-law
resolved to leave
to return from the fields of Moab—
it was there in Moab she had heard
how the Lord took care of his people again
and they had their share of bread

So she left that place
setting out with her two daughters-in-law
on the road that returns
to the land of Judah

Then Naomi stopped—
saying to them
you must go back, both of you
return to the house of your mother
may the Lord be kind to you
as you were kind to our dead
as you remained loving to me
and may the Lord take care of you
giving you a home of kindness
in the house of a loving husband

Naomi kissed them
and they broke out crying
protesting: no, we will return
with you, to your people

But she answered: return, my daughters
why go with me?
are there yet more sons in my womb
who would be husbands to you?

Return, my daughters, go your way
I am too old for husbands, because
if I said there is still hope
that even tonight I had a husband
that even now I was bearing sons
would you wait for them to grow up
would you stay home, waiting
shutting yourselves off
from husbands?

No, my daughters, it would be
even more bitter for me than you
knowing the Lord is against me
his hand already has shown my way

Yet they protested again, crying
and Orpah kissed her mother-in-law
in parting
but Ruth clung to her

Look, Naomi was saying, your sister-in-law returns
to her people, to her gods
return with her
but Ruth protested: don't push me away
or urge me to turn away
from you

Wherever you must go
I will go with you
wherever you must stay
I will stay with you
your people are my people
your God my God
wherever you must die
there too I will be buried

Let the Lord take me—if he must
no matter how hard it is
may nothing but that, death
separate us

Naomi could see Ruth's determination
to go with her
she stopped speaking, no longer
trying to dissuade her
the two of them walked on
together
until they reached Bethlehem

And in Bethlehem they found
the town struck with amazement
and interest in them, with the women saying
is this Naomi?
do not call me Naomi (pleasantness)
call me Mara (bitterness)
as it pleases Almighty God

I was full of life when I left
but I return empty-handed
on the bitter road the Lord provides me
why call me Naomi
you can see the Lord was hard
a stone in my pleasant way
Almighty God was pleased to point me away
from a good life, to futility

And so Naomi returned
and with her, Ruth the Moabite
her daughter-in-law
leaving the fields of Moab
arriving in Bethlehem at a time
of harvest—the barley harvest had begun.

Chapter 2

And Naomi had a relative there
an in-law
a man of character
from the established family of Elimelech
and his name was Boaz

Ruth; the woman of Moab, was saying
to Naomi: I am going
to the fields, so I may glean
the free grain that falls
behind, if one may
look on me kindly—
and she was reassured: go, my daughter

There, in the fields, gleaning
behind the harvesters, she found herself
by accident
in just that part of the fields
belonging to Boaz, from the family of Elimelech

And it happened Boaz came out
from the town, Bethlehem
greeting the harvesters: the Lord
be with you, and they greeted him
the Lord be kind to you

Boaz turned to his man
overseeing the harvesters
who is that young woman
and the young man replied
she is the Moabite woman, who returned
with Naomi from the fields of Moab
she made up her mind to glean
behind the harvesters, and there she's been
on her feet since morning
with hardly a moment's shade

And Boaz turned to Ruth
listen, my daughter
you will not have to glean
in other fields
you will not have to leave again
cling to us, stay here
with our young women

Your eyes will be on the harvest
along with the others—don't stand back
but go with them, I've asked
the young men not to treat you harshly
and when you're thirsty, walk over
to the canteens the young men have brought

She was overcome with gratitude
bowing her face to the earth
in a gesture of humility, then saying
why am I special in your eyes
why are you so kind
that I stand out as anything more
than a foreigner?

Because I learned more
Boaz was saying, for all to hear
how you cared for your mother-in-law
after your husband's death
and then left behind you
mother, father, and land
to come to a strange country
trusting in a people you didn't yet know

The Lord be a full guarantee
for your loving-kindness
the God of Israel reward you fully
with a rich life
as you have awarded us
your full trust
beneath his sheltering wing

May I live up to your kindness
Ruth was saying
and to the reassurance in your voice and eyes
my heart is stirred, as if
I were one of your workers
though I'm not worthy as one of them

When it was time for the meal
Boaz said to her: sit here
share our bread and wine
Ruth sat among the workers
and he filled her plate with roasted grain
and she ate her fill, with more left over

As she rose, returning to the gleaning
Boaz told his workers: allow her
to glean anywhere
even among the sheaves
do not embarrass her but
leave some fresh stalks already harvested
for her, let her glean among them
do not judge her harshly

And she worked in the field until evening
then beat out the grain
until she had a full bushel of barley
about an ephah
lifting it up to take to the city
to show her mother-in-law
who was surprised
at all she had gleaned, and then
Ruth showed her the extra grain as well
left over from the meal

And her mother-in-law was saying
where did you glean all this?
where did you work today?
where is there one so generous
to take kind notice of you—bless him
so she told her mother-in-law where
she had worked: the man's name
for whom I worked today is Boaz

And Naomi was saying to her daughter-in-law
may the Lord be kind to him
who has not forgotten loving-kindness
shown to the living, and with respect
for the dead—
that man, Naomi continued, is a relative
close enough to be within
our family sphere of redeemers

And Ruth the Moabite replied
he also said I should return
staying close to the young men and women
who work for him, saying: you will stay
until they have finished reaping
and the field is fully harvested

It is a good thing, Naomi was saying
to Ruth, her daughter-in-law, good
that you go with his young women
and not into other fields, where
you could find you are treated harshly

So Ruth stayed close to Boaz's young women
gleaning until the barley was fully harvested
and on through the harvest of wheat
returning afterward to the house
of her mother-in-law, the two
staying on alone.

Chapter 3

And Naomi her mother-in-law was saying
my daughter, it is up to me
to help find you sheltering—
a fulfillment, a rewarding security

I have been thinking of Boaz
our relative, whose young women
you worked beside—now listen to me
it is the night he will be winnowing the grain
at the threshing floor, you must
bathe, use perfume, dress
as an attractive woman
and go down there
to the threshing floor
outside the gate

Let it not be known you have come
until he is through
and finished his meal and drink as well

And when he lies down, then
notice the place—
you will go in and there
while he sleeps
uncover his legs and lie down

And then he will tell you
what you must do
Ruth answered: I will
do all that you say

She went down to the threshing floor
doing as her mother-in-law asked

Boaz ate and drank to his content
his heart full, the work fulfilled
and he went to lie down
at the far end, behind
the freshly piled grain

She went there, coming softly
she uncovered his legs
quietly, she lay down

And then in the middle of the night
the man shivered, turned in his sleep—
suddenly, groping about, he felt
a body laying next to him, a woman

Who are you, he was saying
I am Ruth, your handmaid
spread the wing of your robe
over me
as a marriage pledge
and shelter your handmaid

For you are a redeemer
to me

He answered: and you are a blessing
before the Lord, my daughter
you have made a fresh espousal
of loving-kindness, as you did at first
for Naomi—and this a greater pledge
as you stayed true to your journey
not turning, even to the young men
desirable whether rich or poor

Now, my daughter, you will not worry—
whatever you say I must do
will be done
everyone, those who come
to the gate of my people, knows
you are a woman of character

Now it is true, also
I can be kin-redeemer to you

but there is another, even closer
than I

Stay here for the night
when morning comes
we will see if he honors
his role as kin-redeemer
but if he turns from his right
I will stay true
redeeming you

—As true as the Lord
lives in our hearts—
and now lie down
until the morning

And she lay next to him until morning
rising before daybreak, before one could know
one person from another—
let it not be harshly judged
he had said, that the woman came
to the threshing floor

Take off the shawl around you
he was saying, give it to me

And she held it out
as he poured six measures of barley
then fixed it to her back

He went inside the city
as Ruth returned to her mother-in-law
who was waiting
what has become of you, my daughter?

She told her everything
the man had done to her
six measures of barley he gave me
saying: you must not return empty-handed
to your mother-in-law

Sit down, my daughter, until you know
how it will all turn out
the man will not rest one moment
until all is settled
this very day.

Chapter 4

And Boaz had gone up to the gate
where the people gather
and sat down in the square
just then the very kin-redeemer
he had spoken of
passed by: stop, you so-and-so
come over here and sit down
and he did

Then Boaz called ten of the city's elders
to come over and sit down
in the role of witnesses
and they did

He turned to the kin-redeemer:
the part of the field
that was like a brother's, Elimelech's
must properly be sold by Naomi
who has returned
from the fields of Moab
I pledged to make it known to you
it is your right: you may buy it
in the presence of our people's elders
in front of those seated here

If you will honor your role
as redeemer, do it
and if it is not to be redeemed
tell me and make it known
since there is no one else but you
to do it, and I after you
he answered: I will redeem

Boaz continued: on the day you buy
the field from Naomi, you buy as well
from Ruth, the Moabite
who is the widow, the role
of redeeming husband—
to renew the name of the dead
by her hand

and to raise children
establishing his inheritance
the kin-redeemer answered: I cannot redeem

Redeeming may harm my own inheritance—
why not take on the role yourself
the right is yours
I cannot redeem it

Now this is how it was done
in Israel in those days
in cases of transferring rights:
as a sign of validation
in all such things
the man took off his sandal
and gave it to the neighbor
and thus the thing was sealed

Buy it, said the kin-redeemer
to Boaz, and he took off
his sandal

Then Boaz, turning to the elders
and in the presence of his people
said: you are witnesses
that on this day
I am buying from Naomi's hand
what was Elimelech's
what was his sons', Kilyon's and Mahlon's

And foremost, I take on the right
to ask the hand of Ruth
the Moabite, widow of Mahlon
whom I will marry
renewing the name of the dead
establishing his inheritance—
this name will not disappear

And it will live in his family
and in the assembly of his people
at the gate of his city—
today, in this assembly
you are witnesses

Then the people standing at the gate
and the seated elders
said: we are witnesses

may the Lord make this woman
who comes into your house
fruitful as were Rachel and Leah
who built the house of Israel

May your character reflect on Ephraim
your name live on in Bethlehem
your house grow as that of Peretz:
as he was born to Tamar and Judah
may the Lord give to you
and this young woman
a seed that flourishes

So Boaz was pledged to Ruth
she became his wife
and he came into her

She conceived
and gave birth to a son
as the Lord gave to them
a love that was fruitful

Then the women of the city
were saying to Naomi
the Lord be blessed
whose kindness has not ceased
to this day, never leaving you
bereft of a redeemer

May his name live on
in Israel

He will renew your spirit
and nourish your old age
because he is born to the loving
daughter-in-law
who came beside you
and who has borne you more kindness
than seven sons

Then Naomi took the boy
held it to her breast
and she became
like a nurse to him—
the women of the neighborhood
gave it a name, exclaiming
a son is born to Naomi

The name they gave him was Oved
he was the father of Jesse
who was the father
of David

Now these are the generations
descending from Peretz
Peretz and his wife gave birth to Hetzron
he to Ram, he to Amminidab
he to Nahson, he to Salmah
he to Boaz, he to Oved

Oved and his wife gave birth to Jesse
and he to David.

EPILOGUE

I   *A Long, Intimate Dialogue*

Reducing the Jewish festivals to a nostalgia for custom and ceremony is like pretending no one had to die by the shots fired after the original Fourth of July. Yet why bother with ancient history? To begin with—and unlike Independence Day in America—the Jewish festivals do not commemorate events isolated in time, but make those events doorways out of time itself.

On the threshold of the universal, we can become increasingly fond of the present, or we can leap into some great mystery. It's as if the Jewish festivals chose the former—life—with such passion that the past and future are pulled into the embrace of the present. But that is only a feeble "as if." In this book, in addition to describing the festival themes, I've wanted to present the character of the Jewish festivals by re-encountering the great Hebrew literature traditionally associated with them: the Hebrew Bible and its commentaries.

The Jewish tradition is a living one, and starting with the Torah, its original texts are widely used today. By contrast, most of the world's classic literatures, such as the Greek and Roman, have no life of their own. Yet there is no book to present the treasure of Jewish festival texts in English, in a contemporary idiom, together with the history and tradition that nourished them. This book, in addition to describing the traditional Jewish festivals, is a part of their celebration.

Literary renewals give the reader a chance to enter into the festival spirit. For the "Old Testament" is read aloud as living literature—in the original Hebrew and in all synagogues—on the weekly Shabbat (Sabbath) and festivals. Since the language of the Hebrew Bible is vitally used by modern Jews in this way, there should be no danger of mistaking its English version as a substitute for the original—we are free to reach for a creative integrity. So I've tried to reflect the intensity of the Hebrew texts by lending them the shape and integrity of fresh works in English.

From the first Aramaic targums (interpretive translations), made more than 2,500 years ago, when Jews were returning from exile, the translating process has often signaled a revival of interest in the original, and those versions have been used by later generations as a form of commentary on the Hebrew. This new presentation, although interpretive, remains within a long tradition. I haven't tried to reform the festivals, or to construct fashionable substitutes. Their relevance, if not their idiom, is timeless, like the Torah itself.

The festivals tell a story that is a journey from disbelief to involvement, based on the one thing any modern story will always lack: ages and worlds of experience, centuries of refinement, and a passion for imaginative self-criticism.

To be open to criticism requires an ability to hear the other side, and this story is a record of the dialogue that characterizes Jewish tradition. The New Year's observance of Rosh Hashanah begins with the callings of Abraham, Moses, Jeremiah, and Isaiah. All of them are setting out on journeys, open to new beginnings, and each needs the assurance of a voice that is beyond the world's entanglements with myth, dogma, and superstition.

At Yom Kippur, the dialogue is still with God but more firmly planted in everyday reality. Jonah refuses the call, and in the process tests its validity. Isaiah translates the "Here I am" into a listening and responding to the suffering of others. And Job has begun to listen to himself. By Sukkot, following shortly after the High Holy Days, the dialogue has become anchored in the world, a dialogue between ourselves and history. Ezra reads the Torah aloud and it speaks to people returned from exile. Kohelet questions the world's wisdom with the searching eye of Jewish tradition, and uses his own life experience as well.

At Hanukkah and Purim, we're in the midst of the world's dominant powers, and Judith and Esther are models of dedication to the individual voice of conscience. Both take heart from involvment with their people, and both devise strategies of their own for showing their concern. At Passover, we are speaking with our children, as in the Haggadah, or with our lover, as in the Song of Songs. And on the newly established Holocaust Day (Yom ha-Shoah), the dialogue is among the survivors, as in some ways we all are.

At Shavuot, the last of the major festivals in the Jewish year, the love between Ruth and Boaz is revealed as each listens to the voice of loving-kindness within them. The love that Abraham once felt for his son, Isaac, has become the love Naomi feels for her grandson, a proof that the promise lasts. A love for dialogue has become transformed into ordinary human conversation, and a passion for momentous encounters with truth has developed into the daily ethics of loving-kindness.

II Journeys by Heart

Out of the various stories in this book, another arises from putting them beside each other. That story holds a mirror to the year of Jewish festivals, reflecting a journey through time—from the sojourning days of tribal life to the secure identity transcending place. We begin with Abraham, as the year itself begins with Rosh Hashanah, when the "Binding of Isaac" narrative is read in the synagogue.

At the time of Abraham, more than four thousand years ago, a code of tribal ethics based on *covenanting*—agreements of mutual respect—was the context for a leap of imagination. God's personal covenant with Abraham ensued, with its promise of an unbroken line of descendants. This link to eternity in the down-to-earth imagery of legal covenants and healthy children stands behind the awesome journey of Abraham and Isaac into the unknown at Mount Moriah. The result was a shattering of fearful superstitions about death, accompanied by the symbolic rejection of child sacrifice.

Further in time, we witness the entering into a covenant relationship with God by the whole people of Israel at Mount Sinai. And we arrive at the story of Ruth, during Shavuot, where covenant ethics have been returned to the realm of personal relationships, transformed into the ethics of loving-kindness.

The story the festivals tell unfolds a journey to the full flowering of conscience in the world. It isn't the story of Jewish religion or of Jewish history, but one of the inner shaping of a people's consciousness as it copes with daily reality. So the particular stories recalled at each festival dramatize an experience not only *in* the land of Israel, but of it.

But first, the journey with the deepest echoes is the Exodus. Just as the festivals need to be experienced, the Exodus needs to be encountered among the sights and sounds of a teeming history, as well as through the eyes and ears of the biblical poets who refined the story and later set it down. The depths of slavehood need to be felt in order to feel the wonder of liberation; the oppression of individual spirit has to be encountered before we sense the freedom in the ancient openness to a universal voice. And in the process of evoking this history of shared experience, it becomes clear that no simple story suffices. The essential lesson in living the year of Jewish festivals is that there is no single journey, no single life, to serve as a model; there are only particular journeys, particular lives. The Exodus is but one journey that echoes among many others.

The festivals also have unique lives of their own that have traveled through legend and history: from Elijah to the early rabbis of the Passover Haggadah; from the Maccabees to the martyrs of Hanukkah; from the medieval poets and mystics of Shavuot to modern Yiddish and Hebrew writers. The diversity resists any generalizing attempts, just as the cultural and spiritual associations of each resist the primitive kind of easy answers and universal solutions that Jews were often persecuted for. Each festival suggests an unfinished process, a journey, and even in the simplest explanation for children, the holidays retain the richness of jewels, multi-faceted with stories and songs, rituals and dreams.

The modern desire to see history in evolutionary terms is related to the ancient, pagan myths which the Jewish awareness countered: the Exodus is a reminder of a particular flash of awareness at a particular time, and as much as fanatics may wish, it resists being historicized. Instead, the journey suggests a process that is parallel to any time; the source of awareness is always there but must be reapproached. Like the ideals of youth, it is submerged beneath consciousness. So the Exodus journey, like the others associated with the festivals, is a link with childhood as immediate as the presence of Jewish children today.

The Exodus led to the covenant, and the proof of it was secured, again, in a concrete revelation. The Ten Commandments are not symbol or myth but a realization of covenant ethics as a basis for justice in this world. The only festival revealed in those commandments is the Sabbath, Shabbat. As Shabbat records the outer journey through time every seventh day, it was also the example for the process of transformation the other festivals went through: the Temple pilgrimage festivals were to become, like the Shabbat, the home and synagogue observances of today.

After the Roman destruction, the "service of the heart," centered on the reading of the Torah, replaced the sacrificial rites of the ancient Temple, and the pilgrimages and exiles became journeys by heart. The festivals now retold the journeys to redemption through an even more elaborate history, but always remaining anchored to the Bible via Shabbat. The Shabbat is text-centered. The prayer book, the Siddur, is built around the service of reading from the Torah, the central text. Then there is the closing reading, the *haftarah*, a portion from the Prophets that is often chanted by a bar-mitzvah boy or bat-mitzvah girl. Portions of the Torah are also read on festival days, with special haftorahs and readings for the festival Shabbat. In addition, one of the short books of the Hebrew Bible known as *megillot* (scrolls) is assigned to each of the festivals. Most of the synagogue observances for Shabbat and festivals are designed to enhance the reading of these biblical texts.

Many of the rituals and customs of the festivals, in their postbiblical transformations, are also anchored in Shabbat. Some of the resonance of the Passover seder meal is lost if we're not familiar with the Shabbat customs, from the Kiddush (blessings over the earth's bounty: bread and the fruit of the vine) to the Psalms, songs, and grace after meals. In the same way, much of the depth of the High Holy Day texts, especially the Mahzor, disappears if we're unfamiliar with the Shabbat Siddur or the daily prayer book.

Perhaps the earliest transformations of the festivals took place in ancient Israel when the earth's bounty promised in the covenant became the literal harvests in the land. It's likely that the indigenous Canaanite harvest festivals were provided with the Torah's illumination, now that the harvests signified fulfillment of the covenant. Sukkot, Passover, and Shavuot were the ingathering harvests of fruit, barley, and wheat, respectively. The land had also yielded the taste of independence longed for during the centuries of slavery and sojourn. And this independent Israel also provided fertile ground for the later festivals of renewal—Purim, Hanukkah, and the High Holy Days—to develop as fruits of a world-conscious, universal religion, linked to Jews living in a Diaspora encompassing the known world.

The Exile also became a journey. The monotheistic awareness in Judaism had developed beyond religion, and beyond culture, to include a sense of messianic purpose in merely living Jewish lives. The dream of redemption for the whole world was now rooted in the social conscience that had begun to unfold from covenant ethics; and then continued through the flowering of the covenant relationship with the all-embracing God; through the expansion of freedom which the sense of being in a freely willed covenant relationship implied; through the centuries of assimilating every nuance of relationship to the ethics of loving-kindness; until Jewishness itself meant an intimate, family relationship with the world of history, no less than with the mundane world of the everyday.

NOTES ON THE AUTHOR AND THE ARTIST

David Rosenberg was born in Detroit, in 1943, attended the United Hebrew Schools, and graduated from Southfield High. He received his B.A. at the University of Michigan, winning the Hopwood Writing Award in 1964. He was a Creative Writing Fellow at Syracuse University and received his M.A. there in 1966. Mr. Rosenberg worked on his doctoral thesis, "Gertrude Stein and Twentieth Century Literature," at the University of Essex, England, and then taught literature and writing at York University in Toronto and at the City University of New York. While in Toronto, he was an editor for McClelland & Stewart, Ltd., and for The Coach House Press.

Between 1967 and 1973, Mr. Rosenberg published eight volumes of original poetry, followed by his ongoing project in interpretive translation, A Poet's Bible. Begun in 1973, this series of books has included *Blues of the Sky*, *Job Speaks*, and *Lightworks*.

Mr. Rosenberg once edited *The Ant's Forefoot*, a poetry journal, and he has recently become the poetry editor of *Response*. His work has appeared widely in magazines, including *Harper's*, *The New Republic*, *Paris Review* and *Hudson Review*. He has taught at several colleges and public schools as a poet-in-residence.

During a sojourn in Israel, in 1977, Mr. Rosenberg studied biblical texts in relation to the Jewish festivals, and this research yielded A *Blazing Fountain* (which appeared in 1978) and led to his work on *Chosen Days*.

*

Leonard Baskin was born in New Jersey in August 1922. The son of a rabbi, he was trained in the Talmud before deciding on a career in art. He studied in New York, where he attended the New York University School of Fine Arts and the New School for Social Research. The art of the Middle Ages and of the Renaissance had a great effect upon Mr. Baskin's work while studying at the Académie de la Grande Chaumière, Paris, and the Accademia di Belle Arti, Florence.

A sculptor, printmaker, and illustrator, Mr. Baskin's work has been widely acclaimed. He is the recipient of numerous prestigious awards including a Guggenheim Fellowship; an award for engraving: São Paulo Biennale; a medal from the American Institute of Graphic Arts; a medal from the National Institute of Arts and Letters; and the Ohara Museum Prize of the Tokyo Biennale.

Mr. Baskin has illustrated such fine books as: THE ILIAD OF HOMER, THE DIVINE COMEDY, and Hart Crane's VOYAGES. His first children's book, HOSIE'S ALPHABET, was named a Caldecott Honor Book. A second volume, HOSIE'S AVIARY, appeared in 1979.